Psychopolitics

STUDIES IN VIOLENCE, MIMESIS, AND CULTURE

Psychopolitics

Conversations with Trevor Cribben Merrill

Jean-Michel Oughourlian

Translated by Trevor Cribben Merrill

Michigan State University Press · *East Lansing*

Psychoplitique: Entretiens avec Trevor Cribben Merrill
©François-Xavier de Guibert, 2010.

♾ The paper used in this publication meets the minimum requirements
of ANSI/NISO Z39.48-1992 (R 1997) (Permanence of Paper).

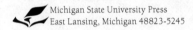 Michigan State University Press
East Lansing, Michigan 48823-5245

Printed and bound in the United States of America.

18 17 16 15 14 13 12   1 2 3 4 5 6 7 8 9 10

LIBRARY OF CONGRESS CATALOGING-IN-PUBLICATION DATA
Oughourlian, Jean-Michel.
[Psychopolitique. English]
Psychopolitics : conversations with Trevor Cribben Merrill / Jean-Michel
Oughourlian ; translated by Trevor Cribben Merrill.
p. cm. — (Studies in violence, mimesis, and culture series)
Includes bibliographical references (p.   ) and index.
ISBN 978-1-61186-053-5 (pbk. : alk. paper) 1. Oughourlian, Jean-
Michel—Interviews. 2. Political psychology. I. Merrill, Trevor Cribben.
II. Title.
JA74.5.O8413 2012
320.01'9—dc23
2011050491

ISBN 978-1-61186-053-5 (paper) / ⓔ 978-1-60917-339-5 (e-book)

Book design by Sharp Designs, Inc., Lansing, Michigan
Cover design by David Drummond, Salamander Design,
http://www.salamanderdesign.com
Cover art ©iStockphoto.com/pixhook

g green Michigan State University Press is a member of the Green
press
INITIATIVE Press Initiative and is committed to developing and
encouraging ecologically responsible publishing practices. For more
information about the Green Press Initiative and the use of recycled
paper in book publishing, please visit *www.greenpressinitiative.org*.

Visit Michigan State University Press at *www.msupress.org*

Contents

The author and the translator wish to express their gratitude to Eugene Webb for his careful reading of the English manuscript and invaluable suggestions.

Foreword

René Girard

Today, the world faces problems that political science is unable to solve. Terrorism is one; the ecological crisis is another. In the long run, the latter is more worrisome than the terrorist threat, and there is a very serious chance that things will get worse. In reality, the two threats are one and the same. If an atomic bomb exploded tomorrow in Manhattan, it would in a sense become part of our ecological problems: the environment would be contaminated, but above all, we would be living on borrowed time. We would know that the threat was not some made-up story.

Today, many people still imagine that environmental problems have been invented for essentially political reasons. This is particularly true in the United States. For want of incontrovertible scientific proof, the threat remains vague and imprecise. There must be a clear, well-defined objective to mobilize the population. Today, however, we are facing problems that are diffuse and global: pandemics, planetary financial crises, melting glaciers, and mysterious and protean terrorist networks. These threats are not due to specific enemies because the real enemy is global overconsumption and industrial development, which, it is true, vary widely from country to country, but which nonetheless remain universal, global problems.

What is new is the way in which we are becoming aware of these problems, which have been around for a long time. In its way, the atomic bomb was a global problem, but it was an entirely negative one. The ecological threat, on the other hand, should unite human beings because they are all equally threatened. As far as practical responses go, this threat creates gigantic problems but, at the same time, it forces people into an unprecedented state of mind. There are things to be done that would entail the whole world coming together to act in concert and which the United Nations, in its present state, is incapable of handling.

The media is not up to the task, either. Even when it speaks of these problems, it always draws positive conclusions, which are the opposite of apocalyptic reality. People must have fear struck into them before they will act, and this the media always avoids doing. There is a human tendency to turn away from frightening things: we do not want to believe what our reason is telling us. The newspapers are afraid that if they go too far we won't read them anymore. These difficulties must be discussed. The political problem must be stated concretely, as daunting and terrifying as it may be. Otherwise, we run the risk of realizing that the threat is serious . . . too late. We need to educate people and persuade them that these problems are real.

Stating the political problem concretely is exactly what Jean-Michel Oughourlian does in admirable fashion in this little book of conversations, a sort of *Prince* for the twenty-first century, in which he responds to questions posed by a young American researcher. I think it will help make the problems that threaten us more intelligible. But I am not an objective commentator. I have myself been involved, with Jean-Michel Oughourlian and others, in forging the theory he uses, which is the only one that is truly capable of explaining contemporary phenomena and giving them a meaning. *Psychopolitics* tries out this theory in the field of politics. That it succeeds testifies not only to the fecundity of the mimetic theory but also to the author's talent, without which nothing could have been achieved.

Jean-Michel Oughourlian is a neuropsychiatrist and a psychologist, but also a former adjunct professor of psychopolitics at the University of Southern California. He has been working for many years to apply the mimetic theory in the field of psychopathology and psychotherapy. I met him in the 1970s, as he was finishing a thesis on violence and drug addiction. A few years later, we wrote *Things Hidden since the Foundation of the World* together. The atmosphere at the time was very different. In the decades since, things have changed a great deal. The shift in our awareness, even if it appears slow to those who follow it day by day, has taken place at an extraordinary speed, which may be unique in the history of our planet.

Can we find a global solution to our global problems? Fundamentally, this is the question raised here. History prevents us from giving an unequivocally affirmative answer. One is tempted to say: maybe. The lack of precise political objectives stems from an inevitable and definitive transformation. The political mechanism has run out of credible enemies because nine times out of ten those enemies are illusory. Let us take the example of witches: knowing that they do not exist eliminates them as scapegoats. Having a scapegoat is not being aware of having one. Becoming aware that the scapegoat is a scapegoat means losing it for good. Thus progress in knowledge does not necessarily mean progress in behavior. Understanding does not necessarily lead to peace. The further we go along the road of progress, of what we call "modernity," the less we are able to settle our conflicts at the expense of a surrogate victim.

Recent history shows the difficulties that politics is having in accomplishing its immemorial task. Think of Iraq. The UN inspector, Hans Blix, was no amateur. He had spent several years of his life handling the Iraqi situation and he was utterly skeptical of the American theses at the time. To suggest that Saddam Hussein was involved in some kind of conspiracy was an utter joke. Why invade Iraq? In order to get rid of a particularly brutal dictator. But there was no lack of his kind in the Middle East. The answer is therefore simple: Bush needed an enemy. However, the one he chose proved to be so implausible that instead of bringing the American population together the Iraq war accentuated its internal divisions.

In his previous book, Jean-Michel Oughourlian examined the problem of couples torn apart by rivalry. The present volume extends his analyses while transposing them into the field of international relations. The comparison between erotic relationships and relationships among nation-states proves to be more than a metaphor. A fundamental insight: *mimetic rivalry obeys the same laws on both the individual and national levels.* Every diplomatic snarl, Oughourlian tells us, comes as the result of a love relationship gone awry. The Middle East feels unloved and exploited by the West. The relationship between them is seen (rightly so) as one of dominance and submission. This naturally contributes to the emergence of terrorism, even if it does not tell the whole story. The amorous lens also serves to shed light on the Iranian impasse or relations between Russia and the United States.

Instead of choosing imitation or desire, as has always been done, Oughourlian endeavors to bring them together. This is not as easy as it looks. It is not enough to add up the presumed effects of imitation and desire as if they were two separate forces. On the contrary, it must be observed that no addition is possible. Only then does their conjunction become interesting. If I copy my neighbor's desire, I desire the same object as he does; I trigger a relationship of complex and dynamic rivalry. The more the model thwarts the desire that we share because he suggested it to me, the more my hatred reinforces my veneration. There is no rational way out of this infernal spiral. The hateful fascination for the model-obstacle becomes delirium, and this in turn encourages substitutions of scapegoat-type victims.

We want desires that belong only to us, rooted in our strictly personal history. Floating desires that are always ready to copy the first desire that comes along are no longer the expression of the inner Self or, better still, of an ineffable unconscious. Understanding the comic or tragic opposition of desires that copy each other means identifying a potential for frenzied escalation that, Jean-Michel Oughourlian observes, coincides with real phenomena. From the apocalyptic vantage point, scattered pieces of data that would otherwise seem heterogeneous can be put together like the pieces of a millennial puzzle awaiting a solution.

This book should interest all sorts of readers. It is written simply, yet without being a popularization. The truth is that in this case, there is no specialized knowledge to popularize. When speaking of politics one can be knowledgeable and clear simultaneously. There is even a rather comical side to this book that does not in the least detract from the seriousness of its message. The outlook for our future is far from being comforting. Saying this with humor may be the only way to keep people from losing hope. Oughourlian's way of writing makes terrifying problems into amusing reading. It expresses a spark of hope in the face of a future that is at best uncertain and encourages us to think about the concrete measures to be taken. For if the situation worsens, as it certainly will, for the first time there will be real pressure for worldwide measures, pressure to which politicians will be obliged to respond. Someone needed to call for this collective movement. This fast-paced, witty book has risen to the challenge.

CHAPTER ONE

Psychopolitics

TREVOR CRIBBEN MERRILL: I met you at Stanford University at a meeting of the research group put together by Dr. Scott Garrels, the Fuller School of Psychology, and the Templeton Foundation to study the application of René Girard's ideas in various disciplines of the social and hard sciences: anthropology, psychology, psychiatry, theology, neuroscience, ethics, literature, epistemology, each one represented by one or more world-class researchers.

Since 1972, you have been working with René Girard, and in 1978 the two of you published *Things Hidden since the Foundation of the World*. Already, in the third part of that book, you laid the groundwork for a new psychology, which you termed "interdividual psychology." Since that time you have devoted yourself to clinical and theoretical research in this area, and in 1982 you published *The Puppet of Desire* followed in 2007 by *The Genesis of Desire*.

In all of your research and writings you have concentrated on the development of René Girard's first hypothesis, which could be called his psychological hypothesis, the hypothesis of mimetic desire, which, you argue, the recent discovery of mirror neurons has validated scientifically.

But René Girard himself, with his most recent book, *Battling to the End*, has opened the way to applying his second hypothesis—what I would call his sociological hypothesis, the hypothesis of the scapegoat at the origin of culture

1

and religion—to the field of war and politics, which were not addressed at our annual meetings at Stanford.

In this latest book, Girard analyzes Clausewitz's thought, and sees the "escalation to extremes," as it is defined by the Prussian general, as a sort of synthesis of his two hypotheses.

One of the most famous of Clausewitz's ideas is that "war is the pursuit of politics by other means." I would like to suggest that you reflect on this notion, and reflect also on what Girard announces in his book: the apocalypse is under way and our only chance of avoiding it is to adopt the only commandment that Christ bequeathed to us: "Love one another."

JEAN-MICHEL OUGHOURLIAN: You are quite right to raise these issues—they are fundamental! I have always followed René Girard, as you said. And if he now leads us onto political terrain, it is natural for me to follow him there, all the more so because I have always taken an interest in politics, by which I mean the essential, anthropological mechanisms of politics rather than day-to-day political affairs.[1]

But first of all, let me tell you about a little-known episode in my career: in 1975, in Los Angeles, through a Viennese friend who was living there, the late Fred Bauer, I met Professor Friedrich Hacker. An eminent psychiatrist and a well-known figure in Beverly Hills, he was also interested in war and fascinated by the question of conflicts. In addition to his psychiatric practice in the United States, he had founded the Institut für Konfliktforschung,[2] and he had made a name for himself when the leaders of the OPEC, gathered in Vienna, were taken hostage by Carlos the Jackal, negotiating their release at the request of his friend Bruno Kreisky, who was Austrian chancellor at the time.

An immediate friendship was born between Friedrich Hacker and me, colored on his side by fatherly good will for the young psychiatrist that I was at the time, and on mine by deep and affectionate respect for this distinguished man who had taught in Vienna, known Freud, and managed to escape to the United States at the time of the Anschluss.

He remembered Freud, who was stern of visage but full of charm and bursting with intelligence, but he thought that psychoanalysis was ill-suited to the world where he was now living and to the patients he was treating. "I'm going to give you an example," he told me. "When Freud speaks of the Father, this word implies, even on an unconscious level, a reference to the Father of the Empire, the emperor Franz-Joseph. Do you know that in all the taverns of Vienna, when the name of the Emperor was pronounced, the men stood up, clicked their heels together, and raised their glasses to the health of His

Majesty? In those days the Father was powerful and respected. He represented taboo and the law and it is in this light that Freud understood him. I confess that here in Beverly Hills I have trouble finding fathers of this kind."

In the course of our conversations, I learned that Friedrich Hacker had created a Chair of Psychopolitics at the University of Southern California. There he taught students in political science the importance of psychology in world affairs. Inasmuch as they are directed by human beings, states are themselves subject to the laws of psychology. I suggested at once that he add a mimetic dimension to the study of political psychology, and we agreed that this way of looking at things was very interesting. I also remarked to him that psychotherapy is a "political" enterprise in the sense that it must have a specific goal and be realistic about what can and cannot be expected of the patient. Indeed, politics consists in seeing reality as it is without interposing the prism of any theoretical presupposition whatsoever.

Friedrich Hacker invited me to present these ideas to the university administration and asked that I become his adjunct in the chair of psychopolitics to teach the mimetic dimension of politics and to conduct role-playing exercises. *The Game of Nations*,[3] a book by former CIA agent Miles Copeland, was making the rounds in those days. In this book, Copeland described one of the techniques employed by the CIA to anticipate the reactions of world leaders: sitting around a table, a number of agents each played the role of a politician, after having read all of his speeches, studied his biography in depth, and watched news footage, so as to absorb his gestures, his tics, and his way of reacting. This role play was obviously mimetic, and it was based on a principle that would later prove to be a fertile one: imitating and identifying with someone ultimately makes us act or react the way he does, and this technique makes it possible to predict his reactions in a given situation. Castro was on everyone's mind at the time, and I was struck by two things. The first was that playing the role of a leader and putting oneself in his skin did sometimes lead to having reactions fairly similar to those he was going to have or had had in the past. And second, I was struck by the absolute cynicism of the students. They were told that they had two options, one ethically sound, and another one that, while better for American interests, would cost 200,000 lives. They all chose the option that required killing 200,000 people! They couldn't have cared less.

I had only been adjunct professor of psychopolitics for two years when Friedrich Hacker's death unfortunately put an end to this teaching experience.

So yes, since René Girard leads us onto the terrain of war and politics, we cannot help but take an interest in these things. But before going any further, let me add another remark concerning the citation from Clause-witz that defines war as the pursuit of politics by other means. I disagree wholeheartedly, though sometimes appearances make it seem that this is the case. In my opinion—and I insist on this point—war is the failure of politics. I think we will have occasion to come back to this question later in our conversations.

TCM: You went a bit too fast when you were defining psychopolitics. Could you give a more precise definition?

JMO: Psychopolitics is an art that first of all teaches how to use psychology in politics. Napoleon compared politics to a game of chess played with human pieces. How could one play such a game without understanding human beings, and how could one understand them without having recourse to psychology? Without psychology, politics is blind; without politics, psychology is powerless. The sage Sun Tzu wrote:

> *Know the enemy,*
> *Know thyself,*
> *And victory*
> *Is never in doubt,*
> *Not in a hundred battles.*
>
> *He who knows self,*
> *But not the enemy*
> *Will suffer one defeat*
> *For every victory.*
>
> *He who knows*
> *Neither self*
> *Nor enemy*
> *Will fail in every battle.*[4]

Indeed, in politics it is imperative to know with whom one is dealing. Machiavelli, too, recommends knowing in depth the attributes and flaws, the virtues and vices of the princes that one wishes to seduce, deceive, fight, or betray. The politician must therefore have human experience and know human nature, without succumbing to any ideological illusion, without hav-ing prejudices, without being afraid to look reality in the face and see it as it is. A simple example: a piece of news or information, a request or a claim, will be judged and interpreted differently and given a different response depending on whether it is presented to the prince by an agreeable friend or by a disagreeable courtier: the reaction will be positive in the first case, negative in the second. It follows that no proposition can be considered as objective when it is presented to the prince: everything is subject to his point of view. Political reality is fluctuating, subjective, made of particular cases, supple and adaptable, non-Euclidean.

Politics is not logical. It is psychological.

But knowing others begins with knowing oneself. The politician must know his strengths and weaknesses, his vices and virtues, as well as those of his adversary. He must know himself well enough not to be blinded by his pride, his fear, his ambition, or his self-complacency, and he must not let himself be guided by his likes and dislikes. Then what, you wonder, will be his guide, what will be his criterion for action? The chosen objective! All of his efforts, his actions, reactions, feelings, emotions, must be guided by the objective to be achieved. That being said, the greatest wisdom in politics consists in knowing when to change objectives if the one set initially proves to be out of reach, idealistic, too dangerous, or too expensive.

It is in this sense that psychopolitics is also an art that teaches us how to apply politics to psychology, psychiatry, and psychotherapy. These disciplines must learn from politics to set a clear, realistic, attainable objective. And to assure themselves that this objective is shared and understood by the patient, at least in principle.

For psychotherapy, setting a clear objective means starting from a rigorous and precise diagnosis. In politics one would say: a complete and realistic analysis of the situation. This means evaluating the chances of success of such and such a treatment, such and such a technique. It also means striving to present the diagnosis and the treatment in a way that is intelligible and acceptable to the patient, at his or her level. It is necessary to remain within the patient's scope of understanding, to know the audience one is addressing. The great rabbi Gilles Bernheim tells us: "blessing the child and the student means knowing how to adapt the essential word of our own lives so as to give a response calibrated to the needs of both the child's and the student's understanding."[5] And that is also what it means to treat a patient in psychotherapy and to be persuasive in politics.

Christ says the same thing in a different way: "Do not cast your pearls before swine." This sentence is not intended as an insult to pigs. It simply means that nobody should be given food that will give him indigestion. Pearls are precious to us, and we might think we were giving the pigs a splendid gift, but they are not in the least interested and cannot digest them.

These considerations must be taken very seriously in medicine; the debate over transparency and the need to tell the patient the truth should take inspiration from them. Saying to a patient, "You have cancer," or to parents, "Your son is schizophrenic," can lead to catastrophic effects when people are ill-prepared to accept these "truths," for words are often more frightening than the things themselves. Blindly throwing raw truths at patients or families is a form of cowardice: the doctor, the psychiatrist, the therapist rid themselves of a problem by dumping it on someone else's shoulders, so as to protect themselves, so that "nobody can blame them for anything." For the politician, flinging a truth out into the world without knowing how it will be received, understood, interpreted, digested, is the height of naïveté and perversity.

That, my dear Trevor, is a concise summary of what psychopolitics can and must be. In a word, for me politics and psychology are indissolubly linked.

TCM: Nonetheless, some readers may think you are saying that politicians, like psychologists, psychiatrists, and psychotherapists, must hide the truth. Your American readers, in particular, will never accept the idea that lying can be something positive!

JMO: To lie is to speak the opposite of the truth or an untruth. That is not what I am talking about. I am saying that the politician who unveils his intentions prematurely gives proof of naïveté. To refrain from telling everything to everyone is not lying. To refrain from saying everything about everything is not lying.

As for the doctor or the psychotherapist, he must adapt what he gives to the person who is going to receive it. He must not lie either. He must not say, "You do not have cancer," or, "Your son is not schizophrenic," but he must avoid being cowardly, must assume responsibility, and avoid taking cover behind the precautionary principle as he prepares his patient little by little to understand the situation and readies him for the struggle ahead by sparing his nerves and energy.

The sage Sun Tzu, who was not American but Chinese, goes even further when he writes:

> The Way of War is
> A Way of Deception.

When able,
Feign inability;

When deploying troops,
Appear not to be.

When near,
Appear far;

When far,
Appear near.

Lure with bait;
Strike with chaos.

If the enemy is full,
Be prepared.
If strong,
Avoid him.

If he is angry,
Disconcert him.

If he is weak,
Stir him to pride.

If he is relaxed,
Harry him;

If his men are harmonious,
Split them.

Attack
Where he is
Unprepared;
Appear
Where you are
Unexpected.[6]

Despite the way it begins, this passage is less an apology for deceit than it is another way of underscoring, yet again, the absolute necessity of knowing the other. This holds true for war and we will come back to this point. It holds just as true for politics and psychology.

TCM: I would now like to come back to the "Game of Nations," the meetings during which CIA specialists played the role of the era's great world leaders. How could they assign a predictive value to the reactions of one or another of those present who were playing the role of Castro, Khrushchev, Tito, Nehru, or Nasser? In other words, how could they think that the real Nasser, for example, would react to a given situation in the same way as the person playing his role in the group?

JMO: Great politicians are people who have found a role that suits them and who play it better than anyone else. They must under all circumstances remain faithful to their character, the one they have invented, created, the one that is adored by the people they lead.

I remember an interview that Barbara Walters conducted with President Ronald Reagan. She asked him if he thought that his experience as a stage and film actor had helped him in his political career and he replied: "It helped me so much that I wonder how politicians who have not received this training can do without it."

The tricorner hat and the double-breasted coat characterize Napoleon, the tunic suit is inseparable from Mao, the V for Victory sign belongs to Churchill, and Khrushchev cannot be evoked without mentioning the unconventional use to which he put his shoe at the General Assembly of the United Nations. Castro without his beard would no longer be Castro, and so on. Leaders create a character of which they are in a way prisoner and their actions must be in agreement with this character: they create symbols that characterize them, and their behavior cannot betray these symbols.

The in-depth study of their gestures, their speeches, their attitudes, their personal history, the imitation of their way of speaking, walking, and gesticulating and of their favorite expressions ended up making those who were imitating them say things that were compatible with their character. One has only to think of the most famous French impersonators: Thierry Le Luron, Laurent Gerra, Nicolas Canteloup, Henri Tisot.[7] They invent sketches and put words in the mouths of the politicians they imitate that the entire audience recognizes as plausible, as "fitting."

This phenomenon, which is familiar to us from observation, has found a scientific explanation with the discovery of mirror neurons by the neuro-scientists of Parma: Rizzolatti, Gallese, Fogassi, and others. I wrote on this subject at length in *The Genesis of Desire*.[8] I would like to come back to it for a moment.

Everyone knows that when we perform an action, putting our muscles, nerves, and joints to work, this action is governed by the brain. It necessitates the activation of certain parts of the brain. Today, these zones are perfectly visible thanks to the PET scan, where a particular zone of the brain "lights up" on the screen for each action under consideration. The researchers in Parma discovered that the same zone lights up in the same way in the brain of the individual who does not perform the action but watches it being performed by someone else. This shows how we understand what the other is doing and explains empathy. It also shows that when we see the other individual reach his or·her hand toward an object, our brain readies itself to do the same thing: this explains learning but also, as a direct consequence and in an automatic fashion, rivalry. If the desired object cannot be shared (for instance, my girl-friend), obviously the fact that the observer desires it or tries to appropriate it will make us into rivals. Shakespeare's plays provide us with innumerable examples of this kind of situation.

But there is more: if I imagine an action, the zones of the brain necessary to its performance "light up" on the screen as if I were indeed performing it. My intention and my desire thus prepare my brain to carry out the action.

By combining these givens, it becomes easy to understand that the imita-tion of the gestures, attitudes, behaviors, and speeches of someone will end up activating in your brain the same zones as in his or hers, causing the imitator to have the same reactions as his model. The "Game of Nations" assigned to these reactions a predictive value that was, of course, not absolute but statistically probable.

TCM: Must it be concluded more generally that we should lend credence to the statements of politicians or of any individual?

JMO: I don't think so. What we can say is that a given politician will never say anything that is not compatible with the symbol that he is seeking to rep-resent, that does not "fit" his character. This makes it necessary to relativize his remarks, and the whole art of psychopolitics consists in deciphering not only what someone says but what he means, and in understanding to whom he is speaking, because he never speaks to everyone: the politician does not address his fellow citizens in the same way as he addresses foreigners, the father does not address his children in the same way as he addresses his colleagues at the office, and spouses do not address each other in the same way as they address their confidants.

You are familiar with the famous adage: "Those who speak do not know, those who know do not speak." In addition, words have a very relative weight according to the culture of the one who speaks them. On this subject, Friedrich Hacker says: "Many Arab intellectuals . . . consider the Arab mentality, which attributes to the written word and to speech a more than symbolic importance, a magical importance, as a dangerous national passion and as a sickness. For this mentality, it suffices to say something for there to be no need of doing it. Words do not announce acts and do not prepare them, they replace them."[9]

TCM: Do you think that Middle Eastern politicians are the only ones who find themselves in this position and that the others always tell the truth?

JMO: Truth is relative. "To each his truth," said Pirandello. This means that each one of us sees things in his own way, for conscious or unconscious reasons. Each one of us has *his* truth; he believes in it, it reflects *his* belief.

Moreover, human beings present a slightly different truth to everyone they meet. The truth thus also varies with the interlocutor.

Truth is thus doubly relative: with respect to the one who speaks and with respect to the one whom he or she is addressing.

That is why you will hear me insist so often on the notion of reality. The real is "objective" and unavoidable. But alas, the subjectivity of each one of us arranges things so as to deny reality, and the various strategies of denial are what psychopolitics takes as its object of study.

The politician expresses himself at a given moment in front of a given audience. His remarks are often inspired by the spirit of the times, the circumstances of the moment, and the need to please and to be elected or reelected. All of these parameters are constantly fluctuating. Take the newspapers from six months ago, and above all the newspapers from before the September 2008 financial crisis, and today's newspapers and compare the statements of the same political personalities before and after.

More generally, people do not always mean what they say. On many occasions, I have seen patients in my office make very strong statements at the beginning of a session about a spouse or boss only to change their mind and say exactly the opposite at the end of the session.

There are also great statesmen who, so as not to unveil their intentions too soon, without for all that telling a lie, make ambiguous statements. Remember de Gaulle's famous "I have understood you" in Algeria? He understood himself, but his listeners understood something completely different.

Finally, there are politicians whose word carries a heavy weight and does not vary because it is the result of a journey that has transformed them and that makes them similar to great wise men. They say things that enlighten and guide those who listen to them. I am thinking of Gandhi, Martin Luther King Jr., Nelson Mandela, the Dalai Lama, Pope John Paul II. . . . We will come back to them.

CHAPTER TWO

War and Terrorism

TCM: In his preface to Clausewitz's magisterial *On War*, Gérard Chaliand declares that the Prussian general considered wars to be "the reflection of the societies that wage them." From this vantage point, what is the state of things today and can René Girard's theories help us to understand the problem of the current crisis?

JMO: Let us first recall René Girard's sociological hypothesis: a primitive community in a state of sacrificial crisis, a community where undifferentiated violence reigns, is abruptly calmed, bound together once more, and pacified by the collective immolation of a victim most often chosen by chance and put to death by the whole group at once.

Let us pause to underline two fundamental points:

1. All of the members of the community must at a given moment recognize the victim against whom they have banded as their common enemy and as guilty. The violent unanimity of all of the members of the community, without exception, with respect to the victim, is indispensable to the proper functioning of the scapegoat mechanism. In other words, the total failure to recognize the victim's innocence and the absolute and

unanimous conviction of his or her guilt are indispensable to the functioning of the scapegoat mechanism.

2. It is the community that puts the victim to death, that is to say all of its members, but none in particular. An example of this that is still relevant is stoning: all of the participants throw their stone at the victim. Everyone participates in the victim's execution, but none of them is directly responsible for his or her death, because it is impossible to know which stone struck the fatal blow. The immolation is thus truly collective. All of those present are sucked mimetically into the collective violence and even a passerby who had no intention of participating will be subjected to this attraction, as Yasmina Khadra relates in his terrifying novel *The Swallows of Kabul,* in which he describes a stoning as still practiced in Afghanistan.

The death of the victim creates a silence of unusual intensity because it follows the shouts of the lynch mob and the screams of the victim. This silence, it seems to me, is the beginning of consciousness.

The narrative of this event by the lynch mob will constitute the founding myth of this community, a myth of origins that will credit the victim with bringing peace, harmony, and order back to the community. This myth will tell how an exceptional being, a foreigner, visited the community and rid it of its violence by carrying that violence off to an elsewhere where it resides and where it will in some sense "store" that violence, the elsewhere being the sacred space.

From that time onward, to avoid the return of that violence within the community, sacrifices will be performed to the god and henceforth everyone will keep from touching anything marked as taboo, as forbidden, that is to say any "sacred" object capable of releasing dangerous violence. For a young man, for example, his mother and sister will be "sacred." This is the incest taboo that is found in virtually all cultures.

Archaic religion is the psychosocial structure in charge of maintaining peace in the community. Archaic religion is constituted by three pillars that come from the scapegoat mechanism:

1. *Myths,* narratives of the founding murder misunderstood by the deluded lynch mob
2. *Rituals,* which commemorate and recollect the sacrificial crisis not so as to fall back into it but in order to relive its resolution by sacrificing a victim designated by religious authority and unanimously accepted by the members of the community: this victim is first human, as in the Greek

pharmakos, and later animal after the substitution of the lamb for the son
that Abraham is getting ready to sacrifice, and finally, over the course of
the evolution of civilization, symbolic.

3. *Taboos* and *prohibitions,* finally, which apply to places, beings, and objects
   that sparked the initial conflicts and are thus capable of releasing blind
   violence again. These places, these beings, and these objects will be
   treated as sacred and it will be forbidden to touch them, usually on pain
   of death. Thus the king of France was a sacred person and the crime
   of lèse-majesté was punished by death without further discussion. In
   our Western culture, nothing is sacred any more: no place, no being,
   no object. We are in a desacralized world and this is not without consequences. We will come back to this point.

TCM: You are right to bring up the Girardian theory of the scapegoat and of
religion. We will constantly be referring to it in the course of our conversations. Since Clausewitz's treatise bears on war, could you specify the characteristics of the war he talks about?

JMO: The type of war that Clausewitz talks about is qualified by the French
military strategist David Galula as a "conventional war." He enumerates the
laws that prevail in this type of war: "Thus, it is the first law that the strongest
camp usually wins; hence Napoleon's axiom, 'Victory goes to the large battal-
ion.' If the contending camps are equally strong, the more resolute wins; this
is the second law. If resolution is equally strong, then victory belongs to the
camp that seizes and keeps the initiative—the third law. Surprise, according
to the fourth law, may play a decisive role."[10]

I would like to add to these "laws" some additional elements that appear
to me to be characteristic of conventional war:

- The first characteristic is that war is ordered violence. Ordered in the two
  senses of the term: ordered because it is waged in an orderly fashion, and
  ordered because it is waged on the order of a constituted political state,
  which declares war against an enemy state.
- The violence in this kind of war is directed from the interior toward the
  exterior. The enemy is on the exterior and the army of the country that is
  being attacked comes to meet it at the border.
- War obeys international rules: laws of war, the status of prisoners of war,
  and so on. We are not dealing with anarchic violence, with undifferentiated violence. Moreover, the enemy is clearly identified: by its flag,

its uniforms, and so forth. In principle, violence must take place only between two clearly identified armies.

- At first, only the nobility took part in war. War was waged by men on horseback, knights. The latter cultivated the values of the warrior: nobility, courage, tenacity, resistance, but also compassion toward the wounded or defeated enemy. The two armies were thus composed of people from the same world who respected each other. The mutual respect of the antagonists is a fundamental characteristic of conventional war. It is for this reason that it was possible for war to be aestheticized. One has only to visit the Gallery of Battles at Versailles to see the luster and beauty that adorned these ancient combats.

- War alone afforded access to glory. Glory was reserved for the conquering general, from the Roman general celebrating his triumph in the midst of a delirious crowd to the emperor watching the *Te Deum* in Notre Dame consecrating his glory. No politician, no artist, no scientist, no professional athlete will ever equal the glory of Alexander, Caesar, or Napoleon!

- From a Girardian point of view, conventional war unfolds in what I would call postsacrificial time: violence has already been expelled. It is associated with the enemy, with the foreigner who attacks and invades us. It thus occurs in a historical, postsacrificial time, well after the founding murder and the birth of culture.

- The values of the warrior rest on a value that has practically disappeared since the last war: honor. The supreme virtue of the warrior was his sense of honor and it came before everything else: "One could not admire / A son who outlived the honor of his sire."[11] And again: "I could survive unhappy and obscure, / But loss of honor I could not endure."[12]

- In conventional war, going into battle, all together, for the homeland, for honor, and for glory is an occasion for joy. Fabrice d'Almeida recalls the summer of 1914: "What was to become a horrible massacre began with scenes of elation in France, in Germany, and even in the United States, when it entered the war." And he continues: "Soon amplified until it became a legend, the joy of the summer of 1914 has become a stock image, a cliché inserted in schoolbooks and taught to generations of high school students. An expression that denotes the era's illusions has entered the French language: *la fleur au fusil,* 'going to war with a flower in your gun,' which means: 'going to war full of naïve enthusiasm.'"[13]

On the German side, the enthusiasm and joy were the same, as Fabrice d'Almeida reminds us once more: "On August 2, in the Odeon square in Munich, a dense crowd gathered. A young photographer named Heinrich Hoffmann was slightly above the level of the crowd. Equipped with a wide-angle lens, he took a photograph. Some years later, he enlarged the image and found a face that looked familiar to him, that of his friend Adolph Hitler. In this way, he confirmed the führer's statements about his joy, his exaltation, upon the outbreak of World War I. The memory of entering the war with enthusiasm became a leitmotif of the Nazi party. It was the ideal held up to the German population. According to the Nazis, with war came the emergence of *Volkgemeinshaft* (community of the people) and *Burgfrieden* (social peace), two fundamental notions for forging a thousand-year empire. In sum, war was Germany's regenerating force. Whence the artifice that consists in rewriting that joy and imposing it on the hot days of the end of July and the beginning of August 1914."[14]

In 1939, too, joy presides over the outbreak of war and the general mobilization. Philippe Bouvard recalls: "We are commemorating the seventieth anniversary of the declaration of war. For many, it's rather abstract contemporary history, but for me it's a very vivid memory: I went home for lunch and there, on the table in the dining room, I saw spread out before me like a splendid main course the immense front page of the newspaper announcing—almost triumphantly—the beginning of the second world conflict. My father didn't waste any time taking his uniform, adorned with sergeant's stripes, out of mothballs. He was impatient to do battle with what was then a hereditary enemy. Thanks to our inviolable Maginot Line and our invincible armies, the conflict was to be a mere formality. We were going to inflict a punishing defeat on the invaders of Poland and Czechoslovakia. We were all full of naïve enthusiasm. We all had a flower in our guns. Nobody suspected that four years of humiliation and horror were beginning. War still had a good reputation."[15]

This type of conventional war—fought by knights, nobles, and princes—gave way, with the French Revolution, to total war and the advent of general mobilization.

Total war is still a form of conventional war but it is much more difficult to bring to an end. René Girard stresses the fact that when two nations are involved in a rivalry it is much more difficult to bring this to an end compared to the time when it took only two kings to make peace: "The Republic is rivalry among all, whereas we used to be beaten by the king, who was alone responsible for battles. This was infinitely less humiliating and made real negotiations possible."[16]

From this point forward, peoples and nations clash, but they are guided by leaders who obey the laws of what René Girard and I called "interdividual psychology": mimetic rivalry, violent reciprocity; in a way, they engender one another: Napoleon engenders Clausewitz, who imagines that he is the French general and dreams not only of equaling him, but of surpassing him, and, I would say, even of replacing him. This mimetic rivalry also governs the duel between Napoleon III and Bismarck, who have no trouble drawing their respective countries along after them into war. The same mechanism of mutual fascination and "escalation to extremes" is triggered in 1914 and in 1939.

From the point of view of Carl Schmitt, what characterizes politics in all of these eras is the ease with which an enemy is found. The enemy's identity is blatantly obvious and the entire population has been nourishing its rancor and vengefulness since the previous war. The French need make no effort to see an enemy in the "Boche."

TCM: As you have written elsewhere, the death of the surrogate victim is the starting point of culture. Before what we could call to, violence was inside the community. Starting from to it is expelled, exterior. In this sense, indeed, conventional war plays itself out in a post-sacrificial time. But things are spoiled with "partisan warfare" beginning with the Peninsular War (1808–1814), which was so catastrophic for Napoleon.

JMO: You are perfectly right. Partisan warfare does not obey the laws of conventional warfare. In his book *Counterinsurgency Warfare,* which General David Petraeus calls [in the preface to the French edition] "at once the greatest and the only great book ever written on non-conventional warfare," David Galula defines things as follows: "one side will be called the 'insurgent' and his action the 'insurgency'; on the opposite side, we will find the 'counterinsurgent' and the 'counterinsurgency.' Since insurgency and counterinsurgency are two different aspects of the same conflict, an expression is needed to cover the whole; 'revolutionary war' will serve the purpose."[17]

In a partisan war, that is, war involving the whole nation, the enemy is not identifiable at first glance, and a regular army that applies the laws of conventional warfare is helpless, even if it is commanded by the emperor in person. There are no paintings in the Gallery of Battles that seek to glorify and beautify the Peninsular War, the first partisan war. Goya's paintings of it are scenes of horror and ugliness, which do not contribute to the glory of the French armies.

Here it is worth citing some of David Galula's remarks, which are a perfect description of what Napoleon's troops had to face when they were up against the Spanish guerrilla:

> The strategy of conventional warfare prescribes the conquest of the enemy's territory, the destruction of his forces. The trouble here [in counterinsurgency warfare] is that the enemy holds no territory and refuses to fight for it. He is everywhere and nowhere. By concentrating sufficient forces, the counterinsurgent can at any time penetrate and garrison a red area. Such an operation, if well sustained, may reduce guerrilla activity, but if the situation becomes untenable for the guerrillas, they will transfer their activity to another area and the problem remains unsolved. It may even be aggravated if the counterinsurgent's concentration was made at too great risk for the other areas.
>
> The destruction of the insurgent forces requires that they be localized and immediately encircled. But they are too small to be spotted easily by the counterinsurgent's direct means of observation. Intelligence is the principal source of information on guerrillas, and intelligence has to come from the population, but the population will not talk unless it feels safe, and it does not feel safe until the insurgent's power has been broken.
>
> The insurgent forces are also too mobile to be encircled and annihilated easily. If the counterinsurgent, on receiving news that guerrillas have been spotted, uses his ready forces immediately, chances are they will be too small for the task. If he gathers larger forces, he will have lost time and probably the benefit of surprise.[18]

As you know, the American general David Petraeus takes inspiration from the teachings of David Galula in his handling of the war in Iraq and the war in Afghanistan. In reading Galula, you would think that he is describing those two wars when in fact they began well after his death.

Galula writes as if he were speaking in premonitory fashion: "The picture is different in the revolutionary war. The objective being the population itself, the operations designed to win it over (for the insurgent) or to keep it at least submissive (for the counterinsurgent) are essentially of a *political nature*. In this case, consequently, political action remains foremost throughout the war . . . every military move has to be weighed with regard to its political effects, and vice versa."[19]

TCM: Since the Peninsular War, which is the archetypal example, numerous conflicts have taken a similar form. But at the present moment, it seems to me that a new stage has been reached with the emergence of terrorism. In your opinion, what are the characteristics of terrorism?

JMO: It seems to me that there are two categories of terrorism: state terrorism and popular terrorism. The goal is to terrorize either the population or the government.

Friedrich Hacker writes:

> Terror is the employment by the powerful of the instrument of domination that is intimidation; terrorism is the imitation and the use of the methods of terror by those who are not (at least not yet) in power, the scorned and the desperate who believe that terrorism is for them the only way to be taken seriously. Terror and terrorism signify for everyone and in all places a permanent threat, independently of social position, of merit or of innocence: terror and terrorism can strike anyone. The arbitrary character of the choice of the victims is deliberate, the unpredictable character of the acts, predictable, the object that we believe is chosen by chance, carefully selected, and the apparent absurdity is the veritable meaning of terrorist acts, which spread fear because we feel our lives are deprived of all security, constantly exposed and prey to uncertainty. Terror and terrorism are not the same thing, but their close relationship is evident when one considers how much both depend on propaganda and advertising, when one considers their merciless and concrete use of brutally simplified force and above all the indifference that both display with regard to human life. This same word 'terror' designates the regime of fear that the powerful create and the temporary or organized fear spread by those who do not possess power, those who aspire to power and who have yet not arrived, and which is directed against the people in place.[20]

The first example of state terrorism was President Truman's decision to use the atomic bomb in 1945: the Japanese army was far from being entirely destroyed, the American losses were enormous, and the "conventional" war could have lasted another five to ten years. So Truman decided to terrorize the Japanese (and perhaps also the Russians) and this objective was achieved by unleashing the apocalypse on Hiroshima and Nagasaki. Faced with this event, which was unprecedented in the history of mankind, Emperor Hirohito and the Japanese government understood that all the laws of conventional warfare had been obliterated, and they were totally terrified at the prospect of a generalized apocalypse: they surrendered.

Here I would like to stress the enormous political merit of General MacArthur, who returned at once to the rules of conventional warfare: showing respect for the emperor and respect for the defeated enemy. He did not destroy the Japanese administrative apparatus and kept the emperor's position and function intact, thereby ensuring the respect and confidence of the population.

I insist on the merit and the political wisdom of General MacArthur so as to bring out by contrast the crude political error committed by George W. Bush when he destroyed the administrative, political, and police apparatus of Iraq after the defeat of Saddam Hussein, plunging the country into anarchy and chaos, opening the way to partisan warfare, insurrectional warfare, and to the development of the second variety of terrorism, about which we must now speak.

TCM: You mean popular terrorism?

JMO: Absolutely. The latter is characterized in my view by a certain number of phenomena:

From a Girardian point of view, popular terrorism is situated in a presacrificial time: this time, violence has seeped inside the community, as was the case before the advent of the scapegoat mechanism. The enemy is everywhere and nowhere and is by definition impossible to identify before it acts. Soon everyone is the enemy of everyone else, and we find ourselves in a sacrificial crisis, with blind and undifferentiated violence spreading everywhere.

Contrary to conventional warfare, in which it was necessary to defeat the enemy and conquer his territory, at stake in the war against terrorism are the members of the population. Machiavelli, after having recognized cynically that "men willingly change their ruler, hoping to fare better,"[21] warned: "no matter how powerful one's armies, in order to enter a country one needs the goodwill of the inhabitants."[22] Obviously, MacArthur had read Machiavelli, and Bush had not!

David Galula observes, for his part: "What, then, are the rules of counterrevolutionary warfare? . . . Very little is offered beyond formulas—which are sound enough as far as they go—such as, 'Intelligence is the key to the problem,' or 'The support of the population must be won.'"[23]

With terrorism, the mutual respect between soldiers, the respect of Napoleon at Austerlitz for the two emperors he was fighting, even the respect of soldiers like Montgomery and Eisenhower for a soldier like Rommel, is replaced by contempt.

The loyalist forces or the occupying army have contempt for the terrorists and do not apply the laws of war in dealing with them. During World War II, the Germans shot the resistance fighters, whom they deemed terrorists, without hesitation, while respecting the laws of war when dealing with military prisoners.

The resistance fighters (from their point of view), deemed "terrorists" by the reigning government or the occupying forces, also have profound contempt for the soldiers or police against whom they are fighting and whom they qualify as "forces of repression."

In an insurrection or a war of the type now called terrorist, the noble feelings that predominated in conventional wars are replaced by degrading feelings: as we have just said, the enemies feel contempt for each other, but also hatred, resentment, envy, jealousy. From a Girardian point of view, in mimetic psychology, the enemy is viewed as a model-rival or even a model-obstacle, who inspires nothing but negative feelings.

To these feelings is added another that is even more deleterious: suspicion. The enemy is within, among us, he can be anybody, even my next-door neighbor. Therefore I have to be suspicious of everyone. Suspicion corrodes social bonds: the English were horrified to discover that the terrorists who blew up buses and subways were British citizens! They stoically bore the brunt of the V1 and V2 bombardments, which were far more destructive, but to discover that some of their fellow citizens, who lived among them, detested them, felt contempt for them, and wanted to kill them, scandalized them in the extreme.

After generalized suspicion comes fear. This fear is dirty, it plagues the population, and it is fear that gives to this type of conflict the name terrorism. The population may indeed become terrorized, and the government may adopt degrading measures in order to "terrorize the terrorists," and humanity retreats on every front. As Galula writes: "Some counterrevolutionaries have fallen into the trap of aping the revolutionaries on both minor and major scales, as we shall show. These attempts have never met success."[24]

Insurrection, revolution, and now terrorism spring up on rotten ground: poverty, humiliation, resentment, frustration. Terrorism is a deferred reciprocal violence, that is to say a form of vengeance. The study of vindictive processes and vindicatory techniques teaches us that violence cannot erase vengeance; only money can: "blood money." That is why I hazard a hypothesis: terrorist violence, which is a terrible vengeance, is soluble in a single substance: money. Instead of spending astronomical sums on arms, let us spend instead on roads, hospitals, schools, houses, businesses, to create jobs and so on. Instead of financing war, let us purchase peace.

On this point, I am in complete agreement with Guy Sorman: "In the year 328 before our era, and if the Roman historian Quintus Curtius is to be believed, Alexander the Great attempted in vain to conquer Afghanistan. After some savage but inconclusive battles, negotiations began between the tribal chiefs and the Greek general. The latter wanted to arrive in India. 'Why are you fighting us?' said the Afghans, 'when it would be enough to buy us off?' This Alexander promptly did."[25]

What is extraordinary is that all of the values of war that we spoke of earlier, courage, heroism, and so on, are perverted by terrorism in the sense that terrorism is the result of humiliation, poverty, weakness. He who wishes to fight against terrorism is plagued by suspicion, poisoned by negative feelings: after suspicion, fear. He becomes in a certain sense paranoid, because he suspects everyone, is afraid of everyone.

TCM: If we go a step further, as Jacques Attali writes in a recent book,[26] toward creating nanotechnologies and miniaturized nuclear weapons, we are going to mistrust the air that we breathe, the water that we drink, medicine, vegetables, the animals that we eat, we are going to mistrust literally everything, and life will become untenable. The terrorists must laugh when they see the most important figures of the West standing in line with their shoes in hand, undressing and getting dressed again before getting on the plane: it's ridiculous.

CHAPTER THREE

The War of the Gods

JMO: All of the feelings that accompany terrorism and antiterrorism are symptoms of the Clausewitzean "escalation to extremes," which is one and the same as the mimetic spiral and the escalation of rivalry. Rivalrous desire is escalating to extremes, which is to say that "my" desire is or corresponds to the absolute good, and "yours" is absolute evil: you are my enemy, and consequently no holds are barred, on one side just as much as on the other, the two sides mirroring each other. There is moreover a kind of "war of the gods": because it is fighting evil, my desire takes on a divine aspect, and thus it is a divine desire. War is no longer waged on the order of a king or a government as was the case in conventional war. It is ordered by God himself, by my own God. The perversion of monotheism can be summed up in a single phrase: there is only one God—mine!

Thus my god, who is my desire deified, fights your god (who is your desire deified). My desire is of course good, yours being evil. Just look at Bush and bin Laden. Bush says: "I am fighting the Axis of Evil because I am good and I speak with God every day and I do what my God tells me." And bin Laden says exactly the same thing. He says: "I am the one who carries out God's will against the infidels, the nonbelievers, and I have nothing but contempt for Western society, which trivializes sex, which exposes women in every possible way, which traffics in eroticism, pornography, and so on."

And the West replies: "We have nothing but contempt for Muslim society, which hides women, veils them, puts them under a burka, persecutes them, controls them, locks them up at home." The two accusations mirror each other! With terrorism comes mutual contempt and mutual suspicion, a deification of desire that leads to pseudo-monotheisms, and above all feelings that on both sides become entirely negative and destructive even for those who experience them.

TCM: Let's come back to archaic religion. René Girard has taught us that it is a psychosocial mechanism aimed at maintaining peace within the community and ensuring that violence remains "exiled" in a special place, the sacred, where it is harmless but still fearsome because it threatens to come back inside the community if taboos are not respected, rituals carried out, and appropriate sacrifices regularly made to the gods of violence, the pagan gods. You have stressed the perversion of monotheisms that "paganize" themselves by mixing their one god up with their quarrels, making their god the rival of their enemy's god. You have underlined that this god, one but partisan, is in reality desire deified, the absolute of desire in a certain sense. Here I detect an echo of Hobbes as cited by Carl Schmitt: "the conviction of each side that it possesses the truth, the good, and the just brings about the worst enmities."[27]

If as you say the sacred has disappeared from our civilization, if the archaic religious mechanism is no longer able to perform its function, how can mankind survive its own violent tendencies?

JMO: Over the course of humanity's history, the archaic religious mechanism, it seems to me, has gradually receded and has given way to the political mechanism. Like archaic religion, the political mechanism has two essential functions:

1. Ensuring that peace and order are maintained within the community, that is to say the coherence of the nation
2. Just as the prerogative of the archaic religious mechanism is to designate the victim to be sacrificed, the essence of politics consists in the designation of the enemy. As Carl Schmitt writes: "The specific political distinction to which political action and motives can be reduced is that between friend and enemy."[28]

And later Carl Schmitt adds: "By virtue of this power over the physical life of men, the political community transcends all other associations or societies."[29] He also notes in the preface to the 1932 edition of his book that the enemy is not a criminal but has its own political status.[30]

The essence of politics thus consists in designating the enemy in order to unite the nation against this enemy, in the same way that the essence of archaic religion consisted in designating the victim to be sacrificed in order to calm the community and ensure its cohesion by mobilizing all of its violence against this victim.

In order for religion and politics to function, the chosen victim and the designated enemy must enable the community and the nation to achieve violent unanimity. For this result to be achieved, the designated enemy must be precise, easily spotted, and identifiable. And this enemy must above all be within reach of the political power that designates it. In other words, the latter must be capable of declaring war on this enemy with some chance of winning.

For archaic religion, the choice of the victim was crucial when the victim was human. In designating this victim, archaic religion was taking risks and had to be sure of making the right choice. Recall the violent debates between Tiresias and Oedipus. Tiresias tries to make the religious mechanism work by designating Oedipus as the victim to be expelled in order to save the community. He designates him by accusing him of parricide and incest and ends up having his way. But I wouldn't have wanted to be in his shoes if Oedipus had refused to admit his guilt or had been able to prove his innocence. In our era, religion no longer performs a sacrificial function. But to the extent that the designation of scapegoats is the only available technique since the origin of humanity for reunifying the community and ensuring its cohesion by focusing its violence on a precise entity, the archaic religious mechanism in our day and age has in a way handed its function over to politics.

The essence of politics, the function that the political power is called upon to perform and that gives it the right to have the nation's children killed and to kill those of the adversary, is the designation of the enemy. Carl Schmitt specifies: "An enemy exists only when, at least potentially, one fighting collectivity of people confronts a similar collectivity. The enemy is solely the public enemy, because everything that has a relationship to such a collectivity of men, particularly to a whole nation, becomes public by virtue of such a relationship."[31]

Another similarity with primitive religion, which had no hatred for the designated sacrificial victim: "the enemy in the political sense need not be hated personally," specifies Schmitt, adding that the political enemy is the *hostis* and not the *inimicus,* the individual enemy in the private sphere.[32]

On the individual level, the Christian religion recommends loving one's enemy: *inimicus*. But the religious authorities blessed the armies that left to combat against the *hostis*, and no religious authority ever advised its army to put down its weapons out of love when faced with its *hostis*.

As far as politics is concerned, Carl Schmitt clarifies another fundamental point: "The political is the most intense and extreme antagonism, and every concrete antagonism becomes that much more political the closer it approaches the most extreme point, that of the friend-enemy grouping."[33] This echoes the Clausewitzean "escalation to extremes" identified by René Girard as the mimetic escalation at the summit of a reciprocal rivalrous tension.

And Schmitt continues: "All political concepts, images, and terms have a polemical meaning. They are focused on a specific conflict and are bound to a concrete situation; the result (which manifests in war or revolution) is a friend-enemy grouping, and they turn into empty and ghostlike abstractions when this situation disappears. Words such as state, republic, society, class, as well as sovereignty, constitutional state, absolutism, dictatorship, economic planning, neutral or total state, and so on, are incomprehensible if one does not know exactly who is to be affected, combated, refuted or negated by such a term."[34]

TCM: Today, we are witnessing the tragic consequences that ensue when religion takes charge of politics. Theocracies take root and, as we were saying, the designated enemy is anathematized, despised, and hated, which from Carl Schmitt's point of view is not very political.

JMO: That is why wars that are commanded not by politics but by religion (note that I am not referring to the archaic religious mechanism here but to monotheisms) open the way to forms of violence that are no longer classical wars, notably terrorism.

Here we see how dangerous it is for religion to appropriate political power. The inverse is not true: Julius Caesar, Pontifex Maximus, consul and general, holds every power, and notably religious power, but he is a political figure above all and his wars have a political meaning and goal. The kings of France and kings in general have "divine right"; they thus have a religious, sacred dimension, but they are above all political figures. The one who took this idea as far as it could conceivably be taken by proclaiming himself the leader of his church was Henry VIII of England, and to this day the English monarch holds this position.

When politics appropriates and assumes the religious function, the damage is very limited: kings have not systematically sought to destabilize the world; on the contrary. It was the need for stability that inspired Talleyrand at the Congress of Vienna. In his eyes, as he tells it in his memoirs, only reestablishing the French monarchy could reassure the sovereigns of Europe. As a consequence, only the restoration of the Bourbons could prevent France's dismemberment.

When, on the other hand, religion appropriates the political function, it becomes very dangerous: bin Laden is a political leader but at the same time he declares that he is fighting above all for one religion against the infidels. In Iran, the Ayatollah Khomeini created a theocracy, the clerics appropriated political power and, as you know, this does not make relations with this country particularly easy.

TCM: The world is desacralized, and religious mechanisms have become ineffective. But can't politics save us? Look how the election of Barack Obama put not only the Americans but the entire planet in a good mood again!

JMO: Today, politics has a very weighty responsibility that we must try to define and clarify.

First of all, note how fundamental is the designation, the choice of the enemy. This choice is the very essence of politics according to Carl Schmitt and I insist on this point once again. We recently had an example of this: in the wake of the September 11 terrorist attack, George Bush did not identify the enemy responsible for this act of war. After Pearl Harbor, the enemy was immediately and clearly identified and there followed a conventional war until the use of the atomic bomb.

George Bush decided to designate as the enemy bin Laden, the Taliban, and Saddam Hussein. Bin Laden eluded capture, the Taliban were bombed but without the American people ever being truly persuaded that they were the enemy. Bush thus decided to concentrate the war on Saddam Hussein. In so doing, he made a political error that he paid for very dearly later on: he did not designate a real enemy, did not discover a responsible party; rather, he invented one. He pretended that the latter possessed arms of mass destruction and was getting ready to use them. Once he had made his decision, he remained deaf to the warnings of Chirac and de Villepin who told him that he was picking the wrong adversary, that Saddam had nothing to do with al-Qaeda and that he didn't have so much as a single weapon of mass destruction. The rest is history and to this crude political error, consisting in designating as an enemy a noncredible adversary, he added a second, which consisted in dismantling the Iraqi institutional infrastructure and earning the hatred of the population.

It is thus just as serious for the religious mechanism to choose a noncredible sacrificial victim that does not produce unanimous consensus as it is for the political power to pick the wrong enemy. Carl Schmitt tells us that "War follows from enmity. War is the existential negation of the enemy."[35] We must add the Girardian notion of reciprocity for war to be politically justified: Bush decides on the "existential negation" of Saddam, yet Saddam was in no way negating the existence of Bush.

TCM: Carl Schmitt's definition of politics does indeed gain from this clarification. Recall what Carl Schmitt said of his definition: "The definition of the political suggested here neither favors war nor militarism, neither imperialism nor pacifism. Nor is it an attempt to idealize the victorious war or the successful revolution as a 'social ideal,' since neither war nor revolution is something social or something ideal."[36] And he adds: "The military battle itself is not the 'continuation of politics by other means' as the famous term of Clausewitz is generally incorrectly cited. War has its own strategic, tactical, and other rules and points of view, but they all presuppose that the political decision has already been made as to who the enemy is."[37]

One could not be clearer. The essence of politics is to identify the adversary/enemy and to ensure that this choice brings in its wake the adherence of the entire nation. In "private" psychopolitics, that is to say in psychotherapy, is the problem the same?

JMO: Yes, I think that in medicine in general, and in psychiatry in particular, the first act is the diagnosis, that is to say the precise designation of the enemy: what adversary are we dealing with?

In psychotherapy, things become politically complicated, because it is necessary not only to identify what form of neurosis one is dealing with, what neurotic mechanism is controlling the patient, but also to make the patient an ally against that neurosis. In the triangle formed by the psychiatrist, the patient, and the symptom (in the largest sense of the term), "political" discernment is necessary to convince the patient to ally himself with the therapist against the symptom when very often the patient is determined to ally himself with his symptom against the therapist in order to thwart him.

CHAPTER FOUR

Mimetic Rivalry on an International Scale

TCM: Is this psychopolitical approach to the problems that the world is facing today totally new or can it be found in the writings of past authors?

JMO: I think that one can see in Gustave Le Bon's *The Crowd: A Study of the Popular Mind* a step in this direction. What he calls the soul of the crowd, the behavior of a crowd reacting as one, leads to conceiving a crowd or a nation as a psychological entity. Freud builds on Le Bon's insights in *Group Psychology and the Analysis of the Ego*. He confirms Le Bon's insights, enriching them with an analysis of the leader as the ego ideal and having the audacity to write: "the hypnotic relation is . . . a group formation with two members."[38] Elias Canetti's insights in his book *Crowds and Power* go in the same direction. The psychoanalyst René Laforgue goes even further in his book *Psychopathology of Failure*. In the forward to the 1950 edition, he writes: "Psychopolitics is to the collective consciousness what psychoanalysis is to the individual consciousness," and in the forward of his book on Talleyrand he specifies: "Psychopolitics should enable us to treat collective conflicts with the weapons that serve us today in fighting the individual conflicts of the neuroses."[39]

In my opinion, René Girard's work enables psychology and politics to shed light on each other and it is this mutual enrichment that seems promising to me.

TCM: In his book *Theory of the Post-War Periods,* the German philosopher Peter Sloterdijk echoes Freud's insights: speaking of de Gaulle and Adenauer's role in healing Franco-German relations, he writes: "It was then, in the talks between the two great elders that the deadly clinch was released which had caught both nations in its spell in a political form of animal magnetism ever since the confrontation at Valmy in September 1792."[40] If I refer to your own work on hypnosis and animal magnetism, the following sentence from Sloterdijk resonates even more sonorously with Freud's: "since that time the spark of reciprocal hypnosis had been jumping to and fro in a dance which René Girard . . . has described as the unification of *modèle* and *repoussoir.*"[41]

JMO: We find ourselves at the heart of psychopolitics: France and Germany, inasmuch as they are nations composed of millions of individuals, behave as two "persons," two psychological entities, whose mutual fascination goes back to Clausewitz's mimetic and rivalrous fascination with Napoleon.

As René Girard reminds us, Clausewitz was truly fascinated by Napoleon. The authors we have just cited would say that he was hypnotized by him. I am not sure this is strictly accurate insofar as I have shown in my other books that in hypnosis, the model remains a model, whereas Clausewitz takes Napoleon as a rival. It is an absolute rivalry that slides little by little from desiring what the model has to desiring what the model is, that is, to desiring his very being: Clausewitz wants to deprive Napoleon of what he has acquired, defeat him and also defeat future French armies. But he wants more: he wants to be Napoleon and ultimately to deprive him of his very being so as to appropriate it for himself: "I am the real Napoleon, for I would have won the Campaign of France by pursuing Blucher (the Prussian), the only valid and formidable enemy, instead of plunging into battle with Schwartzenberg, the insignificant Austrian!"

Clausewitz's resentment toward Napoleon is deep and borders on delirium: in a certain sense, he claims that the true genius of Napoleon, the very being of his model, belongs to him, for he would not have lost the war!

Interdividual psychology can shed new light on this mimetic attitude: the imitator, the disciple, resents the divinized model for not manifesting his divinity in a victory. The reason he wants to take his place, to tear his being away from him, is to offer proof that his model was truly divine! Clausewitz picks up the fallen being of his "God of War" in order to rehabilitate it. Here we grasp the unity of mimeticism and rivalry and the inevitable slide of appropriative mimesis from the possessions to the being of the model.

Certain writings make the same analysis of Judas: he did not "betray"

Jesus in the pejorative sense of the term. Convinced of his model's divinity, he handed him over so as to force him to reveal his divine nature, his power. Judas's suicide would then have been due not so much to repentance as to disappointment.

TCM: For Sloterdijk, what René Girard and you yourself say about Clausewitz and the "escalation to extremes" between Germany and France is even more general. He writes that "it was Napoleon's appearance that marked a fateful turning point in the relations between the two countries . . . his impact became so great, that he created the epoch-making archetype of political genius which due to his brilliant successes fatally sowed the seeds of resentment and imitatory rivalry fed by love and hate, and this in all the European countries he had attacked from the Atlantic to the Urals."[42]

JMO: What appears interesting to me here, from a psychopolitical point of view, is the likening, the identification of a man, a chief, a leader, to a nation. This "resentment" and "imitatory rivalry" are no longer directed at Napoleon but rather at France and her citizens. On the one hand, this means that the nation is personified by its leader and that in the eyes of its rivals there is little distinction between the two, and on the other hand, it means that it is the nation whose leader has crushed the enemy that must try to heal the enemy's narcissistic wounds. The French must be attentive to this side of things in their behavior in Europe, while the Germans, for their part, make incessant efforts to atone for the crimes of Hitler.

TCM: If I understand correctly, you mean leaders are responsible for the acts of their nation, and nations for those of their leader?

JMO: Yes, but usually not at the same moment. That is why Sloterdijk analyzes the behavior of nations in postwar situations when, after the "escalation to extremes," the return to calm makes it possible to reflect. He writes: "after battles fought a culture gets the opportunity to re-evaluate and possibly revise its basic normative attitudes, one could also say its moral grammar, in the light of the results of the combat. The benchmarks for this examination are called affirmation in the case of victory and metanoia in the case of defeat."[43]

In both cases, the greatness of a politician is measured by his reactions, and the lesson to be learned is that this greatness has the same traits for the leader, the nation, and the individual. Indeed, in the case of a victory, the winner must at all costs avoid abuses of power, so as not to succumb to what the Greeks called *hubris*. Political wisdom consists in consolidating peace by enabling the beaten enemy to save face and striving to erase resentment by abstaining from humiliating or showing contempt for him. In the same way, an individual who has just received a big promotion or earned a lot of money must in a certain sense ask pardon for his success by adopting a low profile and emphasizing the achievements of those he has been called on to lead.

As for the vanquished, they must lucidly analyze the reasons for their defeat and draw the conclusions that follow from it. Avoiding sterile resentment, they must undergo what Sloterdijk calls a *metanoia,* that is to say coming to terms with and learning from defeat while reappraising the nation's values and embracing new, more viable habits.[44] In the same way, an individual failure must lead to a transformation, a new form of apprenticeship, so as to avoid succumbing to a failure neurosis or to depression.

TCM: In our era of globalization, what do you think of the idea of combining the "mimetological analysis with the mediological,"[45] something that Sloterdijk thinks is indispensable for understanding today's world of extremism?

JMO: I think that this link is indeed inevitable. The media, the newspapers, television, and Internet have transformed the world into a big village, as Marshall McLuhan noted, the screen having replaced the agora, the village or city square.

Let us observe first and foremost that the information avalanche multiplies individual mimetic effects to a phenomenal degree. Fashion, for example, is no longer national but global, and more Vuitton handbags are sold in Tokyo or Shanghai than in Paris. This globalization has one effect that is positive and another that, as far as peace in the world is concerned, seems negative to me.

- The positive effect comes from the fact that the amount of information is so overwhelming that nations don't have time to be fascinated by one another. Any budding fascination or flicker of interest is swiftly swept away beneath an avalanche of information and images coming in from other parts of the world. This also explains why politics currently finds it difficult or even quasi-impossible to designate a credible enemy and arouse the nation's passion against it: the nation has already changed the channel and moved on to something else.
- The negative effect is that it is now nations themselves that react in real time and "as a single person" to the news that is served up to them and

they are the ones that risk "escalating to extremes" even as their leaders try to calm them down.

Consider, for example, the way in which the Arab countries and the Muslim countries in general take the Americans as models: they watch nothing but American TV shows and American films, dress (when they can) as Americans do, in blue jeans and sneakers, drink nothing but Coca-Cola, watch the news on CNN, and are the only ones who still buy American cars. And what happens? They suffer from feelings of rejection, cannot understand why their love is unrequited and why, for example, the Americans prefer their Israeli rivals. In fact, they are horribly jealous of the Israelis in the way a man is jealous when he sees the woman he loves in the arms of another man. These feelings of jealousy, rejection, and resentment are in my opinion one of the key factors in the rise of Islamic extremism among the masses whose "moderate" leaders, with support from the United States, are trying to keep them calm.

The Russians are in an analogous but even worse situation. First of all, they are humiliated because they are no longer a great power, no longer the equal of the United States. But worse still, themselves fascinated by the American model, they thought that, having gotten rid of Communism, nothing could stem the progress of their love affair with the United States. They waited for the Americans to rush to their aid with a second Marshall Plan even more extraordinary than the first one. They were disappointed and their feelings of rejection are in proportion to this disappointment: the Americans—to their great surprise—didn't love them for themselves! They came to despoil them and, with the help of the oligarchs, to take control of their wealth, their industries, their businesses, and all of this at absurdly low prices. Whence the reaction and the politics of Putin, who uses all of the psychopolitical techniques at his disposal to build up their morale, soothe the pain of rejection, and restore their self-esteem. He has a long way to go, of course, for he must fight against their depressive symptoms: vodka, discouragement, and sterile nostalgia for the glories of yesteryear.

Today, it is thus not enough to calm the anger of a prince or to seduce him. The politician has a much more arduous task: calming the resentments and mimetic rivalries of nations who experience their humiliations and resentments in real time on the screen and watch their models metamorphose into rivals on live television.

That said, the political role of the media obviously must not be neglected. Politicians must take the media into account and each of them dreams of controlling the media in his country the way Berlusconi controls most of the

Italian television stations, because they belong to him. Putin, for his part, controls the Russian media by more direct means.

In the Western democracies, there are media outlets "for" and media outlets "against" those in power. They balance each other out more or less, except when they join forces under the banner of a politically correct cause and beat the public over the head in unison on the same theme.

Someone once said to the great British newspaper man Robert Maxwell that he was a man of power, representing a fourth power, the press. He replied: "No, better than a man of power, I am a man of influence!" This proves how dangerous the role of the media can be: influence is simply power without responsibility.

In our Western democracies, the media interferes more and more with politics and this poses a new problem that Milan Kundera, in his novel *Immortality,* calls imagology. He writes: "The politician is dependent on the journalist. But on whom are the journalists dependent? On those who pay them. And those who pay them are the advertising agencies that buy space from newspapers and time from radio and TV stations."[46] Imagology is the reign of the image that marks a politician or an event, summarizing and characterizing that politician or that event forever. If you say Martin Luther King, you say, "I have a dream." And you see the picture and the sentence. It's a small scene that you recall, and nobody recalls anything else. When the Germans think of President John Kennedy, they see a little scene where he says, "Ich bin ein Berliner," and that's all that they remember of him. When you think of Pope John Paul II, there is of course the image of his attempted assassination, but there is also an image, which ironically enough counterbalances this, which is the sentence he pronounced when he was first elected: "Be not afraid!" Kundera thinks that the image has also replaced political doctrine: "we can talk of a gradual, general, planetary transformation of ideology into imagology."[47]

The danger for the politician and the new challenge that he must face is that "imagology is stronger than reality."[48] We have said and we will say again how important it is, in politics as in psychology, to see reality clearly and accurately.

In democratic countries, modern politicians must take account of this new reality: "Public opinion polls are the critical instrument of imagology's power."[49] Kundera, too, worries that reality may be lost from view: "since for a contemporary man reality is a continent visited less and less often and, besides, justifiably disliked, the findings of polls have become a kind of higher reality, or to put it differently, they have become the truth."[50]

This phenomenon is dangerous. It complicates the already difficult task of the politician, especially in Western democracies. Kundera summarizes the situation in these terms: "The politician is dependent on the journalist. On whom are the journalists dependent? On the imagologues."[51]

TCM: You are right, as is Kundera, to emphasize the role of the press and of images. At the time we began these conversations, the press was focusing on the Iranian elections and the popular revolt that seemed to be gaining momentum there. What do you think of the arms race and the desire of countries such as Iran to possess the atomic bomb?

JMO: The Iranian leadership is exploiting the resentment of the people. The people of Iran also suffer from their thwarted feelings of love for the United States and the West in general. Beneath the chador are blue jeans, Hermes handbags, T-shirts. At fashionable gatherings, people drink Coca-Cola or whiskey, but the country's leadership pretends to be developing a counterculture, a culture to rival that of the United States, and completely different from it.

This illusion having crumbled, the Iranian leadership mobilizes the pride of an ancient people and in the atomic bomb finds the means of defending its honor and earning respect. If we cannot be loved by those we admire, let us at least be respected by them, let us force them to take us into account. The Iranian response to all of Obama's offers for a dialogue is always: "Yes, but first, how about a little respect?" And the Iranian theocracy considers—and attempts to persuade its people—that forbidding Iran to have the atomic bomb is an unacceptable sign of contempt and an affront to national honor.

The Iranian political establishment uses the atomic bomb as an "external sign of power" and as a test of the West's respect. The bomb is also used to cement the nation, to the extent that politics designates any power and any country opposed to Iran's acquisition of the bomb as an enemy. In this way, politics justifies itself because it does not have to designate the enemy. The enemy designates itself and is defined as any person or nation standing in opposition to the nuclear ambitions of Iran, that is to say showing contempt for Iran and trampling its honor.

This is an "indirect" technique for designating the enemy that verifies once more and in an original manner Carl Schmitt's definition.

And the ayatollahs to whom the diplomats express their concern respond as would a lover: "Love is just a word, give us proofs of love—if you love us, respect us, and if you respect us, trust us: we won't use the atomic bomb any more than you do. But if you refuse us the bomb, we consider this to be an unbearable sign of scorn and defiance." Until the West defuses this problem of hurt feelings it will be unable to separate the Iranian people from its theocracy. The whole art of psychopolitics is put to the test by this situation.

The question of pride and success is the same at both the individual and national levels. Recently, Jacques Séguéla, one of the most famous French advertising gurus, said on a television show: "Anyone who can't afford a Rolex by the time he's fifty is a loser." I think the Iranians, as a nation, reason the same way: "What!? We, the Persians, after 2,500 years of glorious history, do not yet have the nuclear bomb? We have failed to achieve our historical destiny."

TCM: If I understand you, mimetic rivalry obeys the same laws on both the individual and national levels. A leader can "escalate to extremes" against another and bring his nation with him but a nation can also "escalate to extremes," drawing its leaders into the conflict or overturning them if they refuse to play along.

JMO: Absolutely. And globalization has a calming influence insofar as it buries the world population beneath an avalanche of news reports that cancel one another out, but it can be very dangerous when it dangles beneath the eyes of the masses what others have and they do not, thus tickling their mimetic desire.

CHAPTER FIVE

Politics and Religion

TCM: I am struck by the very considerable convergences and points of contact that you have underlined between the religious and political domains and now between the political and psychological domains. With the help of these three pillars, which together make up the foundation of psychopolitics, what is your analysis of the current crisis at this stage in our reflections?

JMO: The current crisis seems global to me and it is characterized by the failure of politics. Politics is no longer able to designate a precise and credible enemy, one that is capable of earning the approval of the entire nation. Yet it continues to cling to hackneyed recipes and designates pell-mell as enemies: terrorism, global warming, poverty, malnutrition and hunger in the world, AIDS, pollution, swine flu, and so on. Those phenomena are not enemies; they are problems. Problems must be dealt with by scientists and technicians and not exploited by politicians. George Bush designated the "Axis of Evil" as an enemy but this, once again, was hardly a credible choice because it was vague and imprecise: North Korea has nothing to do with Iran, nor with Afghanistan and Iraq, Hezbollah and Hamas belong to yet another category, and when the Russians add the Chechens and the Kosovars, our problems become incomprehensible.

What people feel, on the other hand, is the irritation and distress caused by an enemy who has not been precisely identified. There is a growing sense of unease, and the doorman, speaking of youth from the slums or kids who knocked over the garbage cans or lit some cars on fire, will tell you: "A war would do these scoundrels good, it would teach them what life is all about."

Politics is thus totally bankrupt, practically ever since the collapse of the Soviet Union. There are no precise and credible enemies to be found, and "terrorism" and the "Axis of Evil" seem in the eyes of public opinion to fall under the jurisdiction of the police rather than the military. Everyone today is beginning to come to the conclusion that terrorism should be fought internally by the police and externally by central intelligence and the secret service, and that wanting to fight it with tanks and planes is quite literally ridiculous, because this kind of nonwar achieves an outcome diametrically opposite to the one desired.

Meanwhile, it is amusing to observe that the authors who enjoy world-wide success today are those who are capable of inventing a credible enemy or "bad guy": it began with James Bond fighting against SPECTRE. More recently, Dan Brown exhumed old enemies who had been slumbering for centuries: the Merovingians, the Templars, the Illuminati and their supposed successors: the Rosicrucians, the Opus Dei, the Freemasons, and you name it. The worldwide success of Harry Potter comes from the fact that in the world of magicians, there is one clearly defined enemy: the dark wizard Lord Volde-mort. Finally, Stephenie Meyer is topping the best-seller charts by imagining in her books a strangely appealing enemy—vampires, who could emerge from the darkness behind us at any moment to terrify us but whom we are secretly hoping to encounter all the same.

The September 2008 financial crisis provides a new illustration of the phenomena we have been discussing and of the failure of politics to designate a precise, credible, and attainable enemy. Faced with a very grave threat for all the inhabitants of the planet, politics attempted to do its work by designating the enemy. Alas! Just like George Bush in Iraq, it failed to find any credible ones, and none of those it did find succeeded in generating unanimity or in making it possible to relieve the crisis.

First the banks were designated. And to lend credibility to its diagnosis of the enemy, politics singled out one very important bank, Lehman Brothers. But the crisis continued and worsened. Hedge funds and traders were then held up to public opprobrium—another failure—and the crisis continued. Next it was the turn of the insurance companies, the international corpora-tions, then of the international economic and monetary system, which, it was decided, should be audited and reformed. A few days of relief and the crisis took off again. In the United States, Obama succeeded in obtaining a reprieve on the strength of his charisma, saying: "I've just arrived in the White House, let me examine the problems we are facing so that I can set things straight again."

In Europe, and notably in France, the sacrificial crisis presented more and more alarming symptoms, which the political power diagnosed as social unrest. Short on enemies and desperately looking for some, the political machine attacked extravagant bonuses and the gap between the highest and lowest salaries. It expressed its "understanding" for the kidnapping of CEOs. Clearly, politics was running out of scapegoats: Madoff was in prison, Kerviel on trial, numerous CEOs had been fired, and yet things kept getting worse.

Politics is running out of steam. The enemies that it designates one after another turn out to be mirages and their "sacrifice" proves ineffective. Politics is then tempted, at the instigation of the Far Left, and in the name of political correctness, to choose a powerful, formidable, and ubiquitous enemy: Money!

Money, says the political mechanism, must be kept under control. Money is accused of hiding out in tax havens. War is thus declared on the tax havens and blacklists of countries guilty of being tax havens are established. It becomes apparent that China and Britain are very willing to dismantle the tax havens of others, but not their own.

And yet money must be attacked, tracked, controlled, submitted to an equitable redistribution, moralized! A vast undertaking, and one that is destined to fail for two reasons, one anecdotal and related to history, the other fundamental.

Let us begin with the first: before the creation of Europe and globalization, money was controlled by the states. Controlling money made it possible to prevent it from leaving . . . and this certainly didn't work as well as expected. Today, computerization and globalization make it technically impossible to exert any control over money. And so the only way to attract money is to seduce it. Permit me to offer a facetious comparison between money and women: for centuries, even millennia, if a young woman caught your eye, it was possible to propose marriage . . . to her father. This gave rise to comic situations of the type described in Molière's plays, and sometimes to tragic ones. Today this is unthinkable: if you like a woman, you must win her love. It is no longer possible to hold onto money or women except by means of seduction, at least in our Western civilization.

The second reason is infinitely more serious: by designating money as the enemy, as the guilty party, as the cause of all our misfortunes and of the sacrificial crisis that we are incapable of stemming, we transfigure money into something other than money or a means of payment. We are going to bring out the diabolical, mimetic side of money and in doing so we run a risk greater than we imagine.

TCM: I am not quite sure I see the link, and I must confess that I am having trouble following you. Could you make your thoughts on this point a bit more explicit?

JMO: Let us start from the beginning: I have shown in a previous book that in the text of Genesis III, the serpent is the allegory of mimetic desire. It injects its venom in the heel, for it crawls on the ground the better to hide itself from view. This venom, of which Eve is the first victim, is rivalrous desire, that which separates and divides, that which will separate Eve and Adam from each other and from God. The serpent, the Evil One, becomes in the whole subsequent Christian tradition the devil, the demon, the tempter.

In the first centuries of Christendom, the devil constituted only an individual or religious problem: each of the faithful, with the help of church teachings and his or her confessor, was supposed to foil the demon's tricks, and to pray every day: *et ne nos inducas in tentationem sed libera nos a malo.* The devil was thus a precise, but private, enemy, which it behooved each to combat *within himself.*

At a given moment in history, one that is difficult to determine, politics and religion, in search of a credible and precise enemy, could come up with nothing better than the devil, who this time became public enemy number one, hunted with sword and aspergillum. Laying hands on the devil himself is obviously impossible, but his minions can be captured. A great witch hunt was organized under the auspices of a special pontifical administration task force: the Holy Inquisition. The inquisitors had at their disposal an array of interrogation methods to force witches into confessing their ties with the demon, and these are summed up in the terrible *Malleus Maleficarum.* Bonfires were kindled all across Europe and he- and she-witches, after having admitted to maintaining close ties with the devil and confessing their perfidies and misdeeds, were tortured and burned. The exorcists were skillful at diagnosing the different varieties of devils that possessed, for example, the nuns of Loudon, and under the reign of Satan, Hell was peopled with an entire hierarchy of devils of greater or lesser rank, with gremlins and imps at the bottom to perform the most menial tasks.

What I want to underline here is that the designation of an elusive and protean enemy by politics allied to religion leads to a "witch hunt" and to a monstrous enterprise of terror made up of denunciations, accusations, and forced confessions under torture, and that the whole horrible machine collapses when, the last witch having been burned in Würzburg in 1753, politics stops considering the devil as a public enemy, and the devil goes back to being an individual, private affair, each having the task of fighting against evil with the help of his conscience and the imitation of Jesus Christ.

The history of money is somewhat comparable to that of the devil. For centuries, money was gold. It was "cold, hard cash," perfectly visible and thus quite lacking in mysterious character, a noble thing, used not for vulgar exchanges but rather to heighten the luster and magnificence of monarchs and churches (pyxes, jewel-incrusted crosses, crowns, sumptuous robes).

The financier John Law was behind the first attempt to create money that was not gold, in the eighteenth century. Paper money catapulted some to enormous wealth and ruined many others. Immediately there were cries of "Money is the devil!" and Law's System was depicted in the era's engravings in the form of a devil crushing honest folk.[52] The danger was clear: money should not be vulgar and popular, anonymous and within everyone's reach. It should remain noble, reserved for the powerful; in short it should remain sacred in the form of gold. This situation lasted more or less until the Bretton Woods accords and the abolition of the gold standard as the foundation of the dollar and of currencies in general.

Popular, ubiquitous, but at the same time furtive, hidden, money is increasingly becoming the new allegory of mimetic desire. It is transmitted from person to person but in a mysterious fashion, it determines behavior, it persuades, it influences, it perverts, it bribes, it is at once everywhere and nowhere. And it is no longer visible. Having your money in the bank is not the same as having a few pieces of gold under the mattress: When you say that your money is in the bank, what you are really saying is that it is in a computer, in a mysterious and virtual space where it circulates freely and mysteriously.

The financial crisis made this change apparent to most people. They realized that a click of the mouse could make 5 or 50 billion dollars "evaporate"! They understood that colossal sums, endowed with a phenomenal, literally supernatural power, were appearing and disappearing without their knowledge and without it being possible to do anything about it, and that these sums were determining their fate. The political solution consisted, as I said, in designating enemies, scapegoats, bankers, brokers, traders, and then tax havens. All of this proved ineffective, and as with the devil in a past age, politics is tempted to designate Money as such as the enemy and to combat it by creating inquisitorial administrations charged with hunting down and punishing not witches this time, but con artists, speculators, dissimulators, those who have escaped to tax havens. Paradoxically, and in amusing fashion, Money, which has replaced the devil, lives not in Hell but in a financial paradise: the tax haven.

When faced with a "witch" who was reluctant to confess, even under torture, the inquisitors said that she had received the power of silence from the Demon. Today, the banks and financial organizations, and above all individuals, have a duty to be transparent and if there remains the least zone of opacity, they are suspect and thus guilty. The slightest shadow of secrecy is suspicious, and taciturnity consists once more in not admitting that you have something to confess, in not admitting that you are engaging in illicit commerce with Money—the devil in his tax haven.

Today, the word of the moment, the politically correct word, is transparency: each citizen must be transparent with regard to the administrative powers. Private life will soon be no more than a word, and this state of affairs is all the more serious insofar as the tentacular administration that requires transparency from everyone is itself entirely opaque.

I fear that, as with the devil, we will see the emergence of repressive measures, trials, and still more horrible things and all without any result, for Money is no more a credible, precise, usable political enemy than was the devil: without a face, protean, ubiquitous, elusive, it can only give rise to persecutions without any political solution being found. The war on Money, like the war on the devil in a past age, will only add to our misfortunes. The failure of politics, like that of religion, will stem from the fact that it is illusory to combat a virtual enemy.

Accusing someone of having a foreign bank account today is the equivalent of being accused of witchcraft: it is an irrefutable accusation that transforms the accused into a scapegoat. He no longer has the right to speak or a place to express himself. He is accused because he is guilty, and guilty because he is accused. This, I believe, gets to the heart of the Clearstream scandal: those who wanted to make this accusation against French president Nicolas Sarkozy "stick" thought that it would trigger the scapegoat mechanism against him and that he would be helpless.[53]

TCM: If as you say the war declared against the devil and the war declared against Money are just as vain as would be a war declared against their common referent, mimetic desire, how do you imagine that we can extricate ourselves from our predicament? Faced with the frightening turn that events as you describe them are taking, has the apocalypse not already begun, as René Girard suggests in *Battling to the End*?

CHAPTER SIX

The Apocalypse

JMO: You are right. That is what René Girard writes from the very first page of his book *Battling to the End:* "the *possibility* of an end to Europe, the Western world and the world as a whole. Today, this possibility has become real. This is an apocalyptic book."[54]

Apocalypse means revelation. That is why in his French translation of the Bible, André Chouraqui entitles this chapter not Apocalypse but "The Unveiling of Johanan." And he specifies in his introduction: "The word apocalypse . . . constantly translates in Greek, in various forms, the Hebrew *gala*, to unveil. In the Pentateuch, it is often used to designate the act of unveiling the sexual organs of a man or a woman, or the uncovering of the ear or of the eyes before a secret or a mystery as hidden as the sexual organs of a person."[55]

From this point of view, by "discovering" the ultimate meaning of the Passion as the laying bare of the scapegoat mechanism, René Girard confirmed that sacrifice is no longer effective: no longer will any scapegoat, no matter how well chosen, reestablish peace by its death, no longer will any scapegoat be transformed into a god in a mythical founding narrative of a culture and world order.

On page 10, Girard writes: "Christianity is the only religion that has foreseen its own failure. This prescience is known as the apocalypse."[56] In other words, henceforth, "Violence, which produced the sacred, no longer produces anything but itself."[57] This echoes what Friedrich Hacker wrote: "Violence . . . claims to solve problems, when in reality it is the problem that must be solved."[58]

Later on, René Girard adds: "By accepting crucifixion, Christ brought to light what had been 'hidden since the foundation of the world,' in other words, the foundation itself, the unanimous murder that appeared in broad daylight for the first time on the cross. In order to function, archaic religions need to hide their founding murder" ("a scapegoat remains effective as long as we believe in its guilt"),[59] "which was being repeated continually in ritual sacrifices, thereby protecting human societies from their own violence. By revealing the founding murder, Christianity destroyed the ignorance and superstition that are indispensable to such religions. It thus made possible an advance in knowledge that was until then unimaginable."[60]

From this point of view, the apocalypse began with the Passion of the Christ, which puts the Sacred out in the open by exposing it as violence. The first to discover the innocence of the victim is Pontius Pilate. Matthew 27:24: "When Pilate saw that he could not prevail, but that rather a tumult was made, he took water, and washed his hands before the multitude, saying, I am innocent of the blood of this *just* person."[61] The crowd then stamps its feet in fury and tries to make the mechanism work by unanimously calling for the death of Jesus and the liberation of Barabbas. But it is too late; the revelation precedes the execution: Pilate states that this scapegoat is a poor choice, that he is not guilty, that he is a just person, and Pilate washes his hands so that there will be at least one person who distances himself from the crowd and shatters its unanimity. Pilate shows himself to be a shrewd politician: designating a scapegoat or an enemy of whose innocence one is certain is a political error that he refuses to commit. The representative of Rome, of the emperor, of the supreme Political Power, cannot add his voice to the vociferations of a crowd blinded by hatred and still not enlightened by revelation. While it is unlikely that he would be reprimanded for letting a Jewish rabble-rouser be crucified, nobody would understand why he wagered his political authority and that of Rome on a nonexistent enemy.

Another political actor also understood the situation: King Herod. He already has the decapitation of John the Baptist under his belt, which he ordered as a favor to Salomé, whose dance enchanted him. This time he is being drawn into the Jesus affair on the pretext that Jesus wants to be "King of the Jews." Herod, who was well-versed in Latin and intimately acquainted with the subtleties of Roman politics, was certainly consulted indirectly by Pilate. The two politicians understood each other and joined forces. The proof is that the Gospel tells us that after the crucifixion, Herod and Pilate, who were enemies, became friends! Neither wanted to look politically ridiculous by taking Jesus as an enemy, yet neither used his power to save him. They were both relieved to have gotten rid of a problem without being implicated in the murder of an innocent. Their reconciliation can be seen as a scapegoat mechanism in miniature.

TCM: To be sure that our readers understand what you are saying, could you explain exactly what role you ascribe to Pontius Pilate?

JMO: "The best rhetorical device is repetition," said Napoleon, and you are right to encourage me to use it.

First of all, let us recall the two conditions for the functioning of the scapegoat mechanism, which puts an end to the undifferentiated violence of the sacrificial crisis and brings peace in virtue of a psychosociological mechanism that is called archaic religion:

- First condition: the unanimity of the community unleashing its violence against the designated victim.
- Second condition: the absolute belief of the whole community in the guilt of the victim, accused of being at the origin of all the evils that have befallen it.

Of course, these two conditions are only fulfilled thanks to the total ignorance of all the individuals that compose the community of the mimetic mechanisms that manipulate them as a puppeteer his puppets.

Pontius Pilate shatters the scapegoat mechanism and thus inaugurates the period of Revelation, the apocalyptic period in which we have been living ever since. By saying, "I wash my hands" he distances himself from the crowd and shatters the first condition, unanimity. By adding: "of the blood of this just person," he destroys the second condition, since he states that the victim is innocent!

Finally, by means of this "active" revelation of the mimetic mechanism, Pilate shows that he is not blinded by ignorance and that he is aware of the mimetic mechanisms that are at work in the crowd's fury. This recognition marks the historical end of primitive religion and the beginning of the apocalypse.

But, with this recognition, Pilate takes upon himself the mission of the archaic religious mechanism, which henceforth hands responsibility over to politics. In order to underscore the power of politics, Pilate finishes off the demystification of the scapegoat mechanism by offering the crowd a substitute victim, Barabbas, who is a notorious murderer. Faced with the blindness of the crowd, whose fury constitutes the final spasms of archaic religion's death throes, Pilate makes a lucid political decision: he will have Jesus executed, but he will avoid making a political error, which would have consisted in taking Jesus for Rome's enemy. Meanwhile, it would also be an error to turn the people of Israel into enemies of Rome, when his mission is to keep his constituency peaceful. Crucifying Jesus will enable him to avoid this second political error, which would have ruined his career.

At the end of this terrible day, Religion has given way to Politics. The Revelation is ineluctable; apocalyptic times have begun.

TCM: In your opinion, what are the characteristics of these apocalyptic times?

JMO: René Girard has shown that religion no longer has the capacity for containing violence. Christianity has in some sense put an end to the effectiveness of religion and thus violence is at present unleashed. It is in this sense that our world is apocalyptic.

What are the symptoms of this world? Jesus prophesies and warns: "For nation shall rise against nation, and kingdom against kingdom: and there shall be earthquakes in divers places, and there shall be famines and troubles."[62] Regarding chapter 24 of the Gospel of Matthew, René Girard adds: "What does Matthew's text tell us if not that such struggles will return, but in more terrible form. He went even further: conflicts among nations go hand in hand with famines and earthquakes, which clearly means that the fighting will have cosmic consequences. It will no longer be the plague in Thebes, but ecological catastrophes on a planetary scale. Suddenly there is a justification for diminishing distinctions between the natural and the artificial."[63]

It is possible to deduce three characteristics of the apocalypse from this text:

1. God will not be involved. It is not God who will destroy the world. It is humans, primarily through wars, through their incessant conflicts, their "escalations to extremes," "nation against nation, kingdom against kingdom."

2. There will be a blurring of the boundaries between nature and culture: the 1755 Lisbon earthquake that made such an impression on Voltaire was

a natural phenomenon. But global warming, melting glaciers, hurricanes that increase in intensity and frequency and destroy, for example, New Orleans—are these purely natural phenomena? Clearly, human beings, with their rapaciousness and their selfish desire, are somehow involved. Yann Arthus-Bertrand's recent film, *Home,* warns us that if humanity persists in behaving thus, it will have exhausted the planet's resources in ten years!

As for "famines," world hunger is clearly a cultural and not a natural phenomenon. Some countries are starving while others throw away their excess food.

3. Finally, I think that the "apocalyptic" collapse of religion is shown by something that Carl Schmitt observed: the theologization of war, the enemy being considered henceforth as an Evil to be eradicated, and of course the other side's position is the same, a mirror image. René Girard writes: "The reciprocal theologization of war ('Great Satan' versus 'the forces of Evil') is a new phase in the escalation to extremes."[64]

To sum up, the apocalypse is the revelation of religion's failure, of its inability to find scapegoats, to produce the sacred, to create stability, order, and peace. Violence is "laid bare" in Chouraqui's sense of the phrase, Pandora's box is open and we are left to our own devices.

But not only religion is failing. Politics is also.

TCM: Could you synthesize your thought and tell me what the essential points of your analysis are, and on what you base your assertion that politics is failing?

JMO: It isn't easy to satisfy your request. Nonetheless, I am going to single out three major areas in which politics has lost its way and which can explain the current collapse.

1. Inasmuch as the essence of politics is the choice of the enemy, the political power must jealously guard its capacity for making this choice freely and at the moment it wishes. Timing, it seems to me, is essential in politics. Now, September 11 imposed on the West and in particular on the United States a timing that they had not anticipated.

This unexpected timing, which deprived politics of the freedom of choosing the moment, was compounded by the failure to choose a credible enemy, that is to say a clearly defined, real enemy capable of bringing the American population and the Western nations together. The definition of the enemy was vague and imprecise: terrorism. The choice of Afghanistan was also unlikely to stir people into action: the elimination of the Taliban was not "visualized" by Western opinion: the enemy was too far away, too blurry, and its punishment failed to produce the anticipated relief, all the more so because bin Laden vanished into thin air, leaving George Bush grasping for an enemy, much as General Kutuzov, by retreating from Moscow, left Napoleon confused and grasping for an enemy in Russia two centuries earlier.

Saddam Hussein was also ill-chosen. Indeed, this choice was seen by a large portion of the West as a political error. Was it a crime to destroy Iraq and hang Saddam Hussein? The great French diplomat Talleyrand would have said that it was even worse than a crime: it was a mistake.

2. Politics has allowed itself to be polluted by morality. The war against Saddam Hussein was presented as the punishment of a wicked, bloodthirsty, antidemocratic criminal, whom it was necessary to judge. This attitude toward an enemy is not a political attitude.

Let us go back to Machiavelli. The prince is never judged on his morality! On the contrary: Pierre Manent insists on this point: "the prince cannot become a prince unless he makes the premeditated decision to be duplicitous."[65] This duplicity of the prince is obviously totally amoral, but it is also great political probity, an essential attribute. Pierre Manent specifies: "The prince's ability to choose evil signifies his capacity for living without a unifying moral framework. In him, the will is no longer given the task of uniting all human faculties under the government of reason but with ensuring that they remain dispersed and broken up,"[66] and on this topic he recalls what Machiavelli says in chapter 28: "he should have a flexible disposition, varying as fortune and circumstances dictate . . . , he should not deviate from what is good, if that is possible, but he should know how to do evil, if that is necessary."[67] Consequently, for Machiavelli, there is not "good" or "evil" a priori, morally defined. Morality has nothing to do with politics. Good is defined only as what is in the best interest of the prince. It is in this spirit that Marina Marietti defines Machiavelli as the "thinker of necessity," necessity being deduced from the objective and implacable analysis of reality and determining conduct that is freed from all morality and from all sentimentality.

Politically, the only way to lend credit to the idea that Saddam was Evil was that his destruction was in the interest of "Prince" Bush, of the

American nation, and of the West as a whole. This was far from being the case.

From Machiavelli's perspective, presenting oneself as "morally" irreproachable and waging war to "moralize" the enemy are thus serious political mistakes that also herald, in my opinion, the failure of politics. Simone Bertière writes that Mazarin and Machiavelli shared "the same secular vision of politics, which must be kept separate from religion."[68]

That is why Mazarin wrote to his godson, King Louis XIV: "Your Majesty must not have any qualms about making peace with people who have done him harm. . . . Your conduct must never be guided by the passions of hatred or love but by the interests and advantage of the state."[69] In other words, the prince, the enlightened politician, must have sufficient control of his passions and feelings so as to take into account only the interest of the state, that is to say the objective that he has chosen to guide his behavior.

It could be added, I think, while remaining faithful to Mazarin's thought, that the mastery of one's passions must enable the politician to see reality as it is, and to decide, if he lacks the means to achieve his goal, to adopt a goal that corresponds to his means.

3. Finally, the theologization of politics, which we discussed just now, invoking René Girard, marks the pollution of politics by religion. Religion has been bankrupt ever since the unveiling of violence and the beginning of the apocalypse, and it brings politics down with it when the latter lets itself be contaminated.

I would like to add a few words on the subject of genocide. Let me begin with an example. In Shakespeare's *Othello,* Othello's paranoid delirium persuades him that he has a rival and, having failed to discover him, of course, since he does not exist, he kills Desdemona to deprive his rival of her! As you can see, Othello's sick mind "escalates to extremes" all by itself: his rival—nonexistent—plays no role in the escalation.

In the same way, those who commit genocide are psychotic: their sick minds "escalate to extremes" on their own, without their victims taking any part in this escalation.

Genocide is thus a psychopathology, a mental illness of paranoid structure. It is also a political illness inasmuch as politics errs in designating an enemy that is not one, an imaginary enemy that the political power uses to justify itself. Finally, it is a religious illness; religion designates an entire people as the scapegoat in order to expel this people's god, which is the enemy of its god.

It is in this sense that the genocidal mental illness has something in common with the current clash of civilizations delirium, the face-off of religions, George Bush's "crusade" and bin Laden's "holy war" or jihad.

TCM: You have just underlined the failure of religion and politics in the modern world. What about the psychological and the psychopathological domains?

JMO: I have always maintained that psychology and the psychopathology are grounded in an anthropological and cultural context. Ethnopsychiatry has taught us a great deal on this subject. The collapse of Western culture, the generalized desacralization that we have already mentioned, and the failure of institutions cannot but have a profound influence on the psychological development of our children and grandchildren, their mental structures, and the psychopathological symptoms that they may display.

The first consequence appears to me to be the unleashing of mimetic desire, which is no longer either structured or limited. If nothing is forbidden, everything is thus permitted and this leads to a transformation of the world: everyone can take anyone whatsoever for a model and thus immediately for a rival. In *Things Hidden since the Foundation of the World,* René Girard and I underlined many times that we are living in a world populated by models who are also rivals, and by rivals who are also models. Men can take women as models and women men. Homosexuality is on the rise and seeks to imitate heterosexuality where marriage and children are concerned. More generally, men, even when they are not homosexual, are becoming more feminine. Women, for their part, are becoming more masculine. As a result, rivalry (mimetic rivalry, of course, for there is no other kind) is eating away at most couples, as I explained in *The Genesis of Desire.* This growing uniformity and the abolition of differences are the classical and obvious symptoms of a sacrificial crisis, itself the consequence of the apocalypse, that is to say of the demystification of religion and the revelation of the sacred as violence. This violence is freed and unleashed by us, free of all hindrance, and in the schools, the teachers are now afraid of their students.

The second symptom, I think, is the fact that our contemporaries live increasingly in a virtual world. They spend more and more time in front of the computer. The latter was first a tool used for work. Then virtual games replaced the real games of our childhood. Video games plunge us into an imaginary and fantastical world populated by surreal and terrifying creatures who are killed with all sorts of gadgets, and who are ceaselessly reborn: life and death become virtual in the minds of an entire generation of youth. But also friendship, and even love: we have hundreds of friends on Facebook, but most of them will remain virtual and we will never meet them. We have love affairs on the web, and once again with partners who often remain virtual.

The third symptom of the desacralization of the world seems to me to be the disappearance of taboos. Nothing is forbidden by culture; the only obstacles we run up against are rivals who "forbid" us the objects that we covet mimetically. The absence of "categorical" taboos leads to an agenesis of desire: just as muscular strength cannot be developed except against a resistance, desire needs prohibition to structure itself and be transformed into willpower. It is common to see the most recent generations of young people, who have been raised without taboos, seeking by any means to experience desire, of which they feel deprived: having no genuine desire, because they keep changing models and because they give up on their desire when faced with the slightest resistance from the model, they have discovered an artificial means of experiencing desire through *craving*. Drugs fulfill them and then their absence makes them feel craving, which is an ersatz version of desire. They then finally feel the desire for the drug with great intensity, screaming and shouting in pain until they shoot up, smoke, or sniff again and are plunged once more into an artificial anesthesia that calms their frustration.

TCM: You have observed this in your patients? And what about a change in other kinds of psychopathology?

JMO: Yes, I see this in my patients. Unfortunately, the agenesis of desire cannot be reversed. These young people are handicapped because desire, which, as I have shown elsewhere, produces, constructs, fashions, programs, and engenders the "self," has not been developed in them.

In my opinion, most psychopathological symptoms can be analyzed as "illnesses of desire," including addictions of various kinds, eating disorders, inexplicable and random violence, various kinds of deviance, and so on.

It has even become very difficult to recognize what the classical authors (Freud, Janet, Henri Ey) called psychopathological structures. The neurotic and psychotic "structures" have lost their individuality to the point that we no longer speak of anything but "limit" or "borderline" cases, or reactions: paranoid reaction, conversion reaction, as the Americans say. The true diagnosis today would be that of an *absence* of structure.

TCM: According to what you are saying, then, the failure of religion and politics is accompanied by a grave failure of psychology and psychopathology in the form of a destructuration or rather an absence of structure of the "Self," for lack of a desire capable of generating it. Psychopolitics would then be the only holistic way of addressing these characteristic problems of the modern world, to the extent that it attempts to grasp psychological and politico-religious problems in their reciprocal imbrications and determinisms.

JMO: Yes, I think so, and that is perhaps what makes these conversations worthwhile.

CHAPTER SEVEN

Is There Any Hope?

TCM: We have just described the symptoms of the apocalypse, or at least some of them. Given this clinical profile, do you think it is possible to suggest a treatment, and is there any hope of preventing the apocalypse from taking on the meaning that it has in most people's minds, namely "the end of the world"?

JMO: As you know, once the diagnosis has been made, there is no hope of a cure unless the patient cooperates in the treatment. The gravity of the situation comes from the fact that the vast majority of humans are absolutely unaware that there is a problem, while those who are capable of such awareness are in denial or wallow complacently in their illness. In *Le Cid* (act 2, scene 5), Corneille captured this state of mind:

> *When a sick woman loves her sickness, she's*
> *Unlikely to respond to remedies!*[70]

And yet, the whole planet is aware that it must unite. That is what Barack Obama said in Strasbourg to an audience of thousands of French and German students. He said that the planet would have to come together in order to change the world. But the eternal, millennial mechanism that consists in searching for a scapegoat or a precise enemy that will give politics some leverage on the real is lacking in strength, as you said, and can't be put into action.

How can the apocalypse be avoided given the upsurge of violence, violence that no longer has an outlet, and the rise of destructive technology? Given a lack of scapegoats, which appear to be multiplying but which in reality are ineffective because they are no longer of the same quality as the good old scapegoats of the past? Given the failure of politics, what are we to do to avoid the apocalypse? There is perhaps only one solution left, one that Plato and a few other philosophers imagined long ago: a leader or a politician who is an enlightened sage and who guides his people along the road to wisdom. And what does wisdom mean in the case that concerns us? It means waging a struggle against oneself. Indeed, if you tell someone that he must fight himself, you have found a clearly identified enemy. By encouraging people to overcome their rivalries, to struggle with themselves and to transform themselves individually, I think that it would be possible to channel and harness violence, but this requires great wisdom at the head of the state, which in turn implies a great deal of personal effort, a type of asceticism. I have begun to attempt something similar in my own little domain. Having learned to exert greater control over myself, an undertaking that required time and effort, and which is for that matter far from being complete, I have observed that when I invite my patients to fight against their passions, their drives, against the interpersonal mechanisms and inner urges of which they are victim, I manage to mobilize their energies and enable them to deflect their violence away from exterior objects. This is perhaps the only solution, because it is no longer possible to find a single enemy today that is sufficiently precise and clearly identified, except maybe the Martians! We would have to find extraterrestrials in order to mobilize humanity against a truly common enemy. Alas, the extraterrestrials are conspicuous by their absence, except in a few science fiction movies.

It is a solution that I call political or psychopolitical, but in fact it is "initiatory." Every initiation rite on the planet aims at precisely that: the transformation of the self. That is what Mircea Eliade says: initiation is a ritual agony, death, and resurrection. Here we have all of the ingredients necessary for evacuating violence in the experience of death and the experience of resurrection, but everything happens within the self, thus without material harm. And it is by encouraging everyone to undergo this initiation, this self-transformation, this struggle of each against his or her own urges, that we can change the world.

What is necessary is that politics define this undertaking as being the ideal one, so as to encourage as many people as possible to engage in it. The solution is to find the enemy in oneself, and to say to people, the greatest and the only victory that you can achieve is victory over yourself. Do not seek to win victories over others.

Moreover, victory over oneself is the only one that is not bloody, that makes no victims, that produces only winners. It is also a victory that opens the way to other victories, the next goal to be achieved coming into view with each new stage in the process.

TCM: This is what Sloterdijk called a metanoia, employing a word used in the Bible that means "conversion."

JMO: We come back to conversion, the conversion of each to this new combat that is an interior combat instead of being an exterior combat. I believe that this is the only timely, surprising, unexpected, and innovative solution, which states the problem in an entirely new way.

It is a question of making a 180-degree about-face, because what human beings have always done is to look for scapegoats that they can expel and in this way purify themselves of their violence and live in peace. This mechanism is safeguarded by archaic religions, but we explained above that these religions have been failing since the revelation of their founding mechanism by the Passion.

We have also explained the failure of politics, which is currently unable to find a credible, precise enemy capable of revitalizing the nation.

Psychology has always tried to have recourse to a similar kind of recipe: expulsion. Before recent developments in science, physical medicine had recourse for centuries to purgatives, enemas, and bloodlettings to evacuate illness from the organism.

Let me explain briefly what happened in psychology and psychopathology. From the earliest times, doctors noticed that there was, in men as in women, an "other endowed with a life of its own," as the felicitous expression of Aretaeus of Cappadocia would have it. This was obvious for the male member, which led its own "life," without its owner's consent and without the brain being able to exert any voluntary influence over it. Where women were concerned, the uterus and the adnexa (ovaries, fallopian tubes) were considered to be a capricious animal, which often escaped from the lower abdomen toward the lungs and the throat, thus explaining all of the symptoms of suffocation, nervous crises, and fainting fits in women who would later be called hysterics, from *hystera*, the Greek word for "womb." This other, the sexual organs, was thus a pathogenic other. It was precise, clearly designated, but obviously could not be expelled: treatment thus consisted in calming it, and the essential prescription was marriage, with, over the course of the centuries, some more imaginative prescriptions as well from time to time, which I discussed in *The Puppet of Desire*.

With Saint Augustine, the pathogenic other, the other-as-source-of-evil, could no longer be considered as an intraphysical other created by God. The accusation was thus leveled at the demon, that is to say an extrapsychic other, which exorcists would continue to expel from the bodies of the possessed for centuries.

Finally, with Mesmer, Puységur, Janet, and Freud, the pathogenic other was located within the subject and individualized in the form of the unconscious. This time, the intrapsychic other could not be expelled, but was rather evacuated little by little through psychoanalysis, which undertook to limit its unhealthy effects by gradually bringing repressed memories to the surface.

In my previous books, I tried to show that when mimetic and interdividual psychology burst onto the scene, they rendered all of these approaches obsolete. The other who causes us problems is a real, exterior other, and the era of relational psychopathology has begun. The only solution to the mimetic conflicts and rivalries that make us their puppets is to look at the real and, by means of mimetic initiation, to arrive at a vision of our reactions and our relationships that is lucid enough to enable us to overcome those conflicts and rivalries.

This means that the failure of religion due to a lack of scapegoats and the failure of politics due to a lack of precise and credible enemies are accompanied by the failure of classical psychology and psychopathology due to the end of this parade of imaginary others held responsible for all our misfortunes, whether these others were intraphysical, extrapsychic, or intrapsychic.

That is why I think that religion, politics, and psychology, brought together under the banner of psychopolitics, can have but one message: discover, each of you, the mechanisms of which you are the plaything, the mechanisms that create rivals for you and antagonize those around you; change the way you see the world and, thanks to a process of initiation, learn to see reality as it is: the path of wisdom is the only one that can lead us away from the apocalypse in the everyday sense of the term.

TCM: What characterizes the three failures that you just cited?

JMO: The failure of religion is fanaticism and murderous madness, the escalation to extremes in the name of God and at the behest of religion, and in our time it is also, alas, the justification of terrorism. We called that the war of the gods a bit earlier.

The failure of politics is war, as I already said. But it is also, in a more discreet way, administrative matters creeping into the political sphere. Recently, Barack Obama used the word "stupid" to describe a policeman who had arrested one of his friends, a professor at Harvard. He left his political role and got mixed up in an incident that should have led to routine disciplinary action. The same can be said of all politicians who lower themselves by leaving the sacred heights where they should reside and dealing with some particular administrative case.

TCM: And what do you mean by "reality," which you mention frequently and which, you say, we must learn to see by radically changing our perspective. If I understand you correctly, the failure of psychology is the misrecognition and denial of the Real.

JMO: In a previous book, I insisted on the fact that desire and rivalry are born together, that they emerge together from the tree forbidden by God in the earthly paradise. Desire is not born of the object, but of the other. It is copied from the other's desire. It is mimetic. And thus rivalrous.

Do you know what word the Spanish often use for desire? *Ilusión.* Contagious mimetic desire—that is, suggested to me by another—is indeed an illusion. And thus the rivalry that derives from it is also an illusion. Radically changing one's perspective means "seeing" this illusion, understanding that desire and rivalry must be gotten rid of in order to see reality. Krishnamurti's entire oeuvre recommends the discovery of the real and it is interesting to reread it in light of the mimetic theory.

In this sense, seeing reality, discovering the real, means rendering conflict null and void, making rivalries empty and dull.

TCM: You are in agreement with René Girard about the need to eliminate conflicts and rivalries, and obviously that doesn't surprise me. But concretely speaking, could you give me one example of an enterprise that could guide politics and that would go in that direction?

JMO: In thinking about the state of mind and the motivation of people at work, I was enlightened by Charles Péguy's fable of the stonecutters, which my friend Boris Cyrulnik often recounts.[71] Péguy was going on a pilgrimage to Chartres. He saw a tired, sweating man who was cutting stones. He approached him:

"What are you doing, sir?"

"As you can see, I am cutting stones. It's hard, my back hurts, I'm thirsty, I'm hot. My job is worthless, and so am I."

Péguy continued on his way and saw further down the road another man who was cutting stones and who didn't seem quite so unhappy.

"Sir, what are you doing?"

"Well, I'm earning a living. I'm cutting stones. It was the only job I could find to feed my family, and I'm quite happy to have it."

Walking along, Péguy approached a third stonecutter. This one was smiling, radiant, and welcomed him with good humor. Seeing Péguy's surprise, he said:

"Sir, I am building a cathedral!"

In all three cases, it's the same work, but the *meaning* given to the work is totally different. Forced labor in the first case, lacking in meaning and thus degrading and devalued. In the second case, a good job for feeding the family and thus esteemed and useful. In the third case, exalted and exalting work, work that is directed toward a meaningful goal. Milan Kundera confirms this in *Slowness*: "we scientific folk are privileged, for to do work that is also our passion is a privilege."[72]

An initiatory dimension emerges as soon as work is given direction and situated in time. This directedness gives hope and confers on work a sacred meaning that encourages faith. One cuts stones in a different way when one has a cathedral in mind! Moreover, a cathedral is not built by one person, but with companions who all have the same goal and who motivate one another. The work has direction, a transcendent meaning and a goal. It is undertaken in a spirit of faith and hope because the majority of workers on the site know that they will never see the cathedral finished in their lifetime. But it is above all initiatory, transformative work in the sense that it changes not only the environment, in the Hegelian sense of the term, by giving form and meaning to a bunch of stones, but above all the people who are working, who notice to their great surprise that they are being transformed themselves, that they are evolving and changing as the edifice rises up, that the transformation of the environment through work leads to a profound transformation of their very being, an initiatory experience.

There is this collective work, but there is also the individual work that enthralls the painter in his studio, the sculptor, the researcher in his laboratory, the doctor or the psychotherapist in his office, and this kind of fascinating, engrossing work, which is the worker's whole life, is equally initiatory inasmuch as the one who does it is little by little transformed. I should also mention the admirable work of people like the Abbé Pierre, Sister Emmanuelle, and Mother Teresa, who devoted their lives completely to others, working night and day, tirelessly, without any motivation but their faith.

Having said all of this, you ask me what politics can do in this particular case: promote work, this kind of work. That is to say, separate the work from the job. A job is a contract; work is a passion. Everyone who works in the way I have just described should be spared from doing a job. A means of helping them must be found, a means of supporting them and respecting their occupation and above all a means of letting them work without bureaucratic distractions.

Understood in this way, it is clear that work is a protection against the temptation to wage war (the failure of politics), that it is a protection against fanaticism (the failure of religion), and that it is a protection against neurosis and psychosis (the failure of psychology).

Politics cannot force people to work in this way, but it can and must respect, help, and protect those who do work in this way.

Jobs are something else, because creating jobs in the current French understanding of the word job means creating a short- or long-term contract that makes it possible for someone to go to work every morning saying: "How boring this is, how stressful and how exhausting," and to dream of nothing but three things: some winter holidays to go skiing, a good summer vacation, and retirement as soon as possible. And the last few years have demonstrated that this is so. So in fact, it is not jobs that must be created, but rather work capable of raising people up and filling them with enthusiasm. The scenario would be to create the conditions necessary for transforming jobs into work. This would necessitate some value-adding administrative measures, continuous instruction, and recurring explanations of the meaning and the goal of what people are doing, clear objectives, and compensation for effort and talent, and perhaps also what General de Gaulle called "participation," that is, making all workers shareholders of their company. Finally, and perhaps above all, it would mean having respect for everyone's position and occupation, regardless of what they earn.

It is sad, unfortunate, and dangerous to reduce the life of a man or a woman to a *job*: they are happy to be able to feed their family, but that doesn't give any meaning to their lives. Their lives consist of waiting for death, that is to say waiting to retire, which is a little death that supposedly makes it possible to start taking advantage of life. But I notice that everyone who goes into retirement is depressed. They wanted to do a lot of things, but the only tragedy is that because they are depressed they no longer have any drive to do them.

Everyone's occupation must have meaning and be integrated into the group's activities so that it has meaning not only on its own but also one that fits into the group. Some find meaning in their work in apparent solitude: Picasso was alone in his studio, but living with him were all the masters whose works he knew by heart and from whom he drew inspiration, obviously with changes that transformed his "imitations" into original works, into Picassos. Let us recall here that imitation both adds and subtracts information from the model being imitated!

TCM: Let's talk about what we called metanoia or conversion. How does that work concretely, what are the stages in the process? When you try to help patients get rid of the mimetic mechanism that is manipulating them, what must they do?

JMO: The first thing to do is always the same: look reality in the face. I would say that there is a series of conversions, but the first one involves radically changing one's perspective, which for the patient consists in seeing, in a very exact way, the mechanisms of which he or she is the plaything. This can happen fairly quickly in certain cases, when, for example, the patient has marital problems. But first of all the patient must agree to look at reality as it is and not as he imagines it in his dreams or as he used to imagine it, even if it is distressing and upsetting to see reality this way. There are people who refuse to recognize that the woman they married is not a paragon of kindness and virtue. There are women who refuse to admit that their husband is an alcoholic, that he's lazy. The first thing is to look at the reality inside of you, in front of you, and between you and the other person, because it is in relationship with others that psychological reality is manifested. Often, what prevents people from "seeing" is some kind of pseudo-morality. "If I see that my husband is drinking, I am judging him, because it's bad to drink, and I am condemning him. I cannot bring myself to do that." What this woman needs to hear is that seeing reality does not mean passing judgment, but rather understanding. Morality has no more place in psychology than it does in politics. Once you have radically changed your perspective, once you have *seen,* I think that the problem is already on its way to being resolved, provided you see things as they really are. And then there is the fact of being willing to do everything possible, not exactly to gain mastery over reality—mastery isn't the right word—but to get around or deal with or live with that reality, and not everyone is capable of that. For example, in a couple, if you see that the origin of the conflict is a rivalry, and that as a result the woman or the man can't stand to be wrong, the other person, the one who has come to see you, must agree to tell the spouse, "You're right" every time. But many people refuse to do that. They say: "But how can I tell that imbecile that he's right— he's wrong!" But I say: "But tell him that he's right anyway. What's the big deal? The words that you are going to utter have no importance, what people say has no importance." People seem to think that as soon as they open their mouths whatever comes out is tremendously important.

A man told me: "I want my wife to know that I'm still a hit with the ladies. I don't want her to think that nobody is interested in me. You know, I took a business trip the other day and she got all angry because she suspected me of having taken some time off to go out on the town—and I didn't deny it. I told her that plenty of women, and one woman in particular, seemed to find me quite handsome!" And he said: "Ever since, her attitude toward me has changed and the situation has become quite bad." I said to him: "My dear fellow, this is not good, you are going to stir up her mimetic rivalry, her jealousy, you are going to stir up several things that will make your life hell. If you want to have a peaceful marriage, I'm telling you, get it into your head to say: 'I'm old, I'm tired, and nobody finds me seductive.'" And he said to me: "No! That's not true at all! I could never tell her that." And there was no way to convince him. There are people who will not submit to reality. And there are those, who, on the contrary, accept it. There is an English play by Oliver Goldsmith called *She Stoops to Conquer* (1773), in which an upper-class girl pretends to be less wealthy and refined than she really is in order to bring out the best in her suitor. It is this kind of attitude that you have to help some people understand where couples are concerned. And it's very difficult to understand, because most people think that telling their wife, "I won, my boss congratulated me, women go crazy as soon as I walk in the room, they think I'm wonderful," is going to make her happy. They think she's going to say: "I married a great guy." But just the opposite happens! The woman says to herself: "Just who does this cretin think he is?"

TCM: Can you think of some historical examples of politicians who used the techniques that you recommend? That is to say, if I have understood you correctly, politicians who have designated a precise enemy whose designation disarms violence: oneself. In short, politicians who encourage their nations to undergo conversion, *metanoia,* to avoid violence by transforming themselves over the course of an initiatory process?

JMO: I am going to give you three examples that are rather different from each other. The first one is the Dalai Lama. You will tell me that the fact that he emphasizes spirituality, nonviolence, metamorphosis, gradual initiation, and so on, and not at all armed struggle against the Chinese means that he has failed because in fact the Chinese conquered Tibet. It is much easier to hear the fanatics who scream like madmen on street corners or on television than it is to hear sages who are saying calming, peaceful things. The Dalai Lama may have failed on a local level. But Tibet continues to exist. And Tibet has never before been supported by so many people in the world. Today, Tibet is recognized, the Dalai Lama is recognized without having fired a single shot, he visits all the world leaders, and the Tibetan cause is very popular all over the world. So it cannot be said that he's been a total failure. And yet the Dalai Lama has never asked anyone to fire a single shot at the Chinese; rather, he has asked people to work on improving themselves so as to achieve personal growth and bring themselves closer to the divine, so as to keep alive *within themselves* the faith and culture of the Tibetan people.

The second example is Gandhi. He identified the enemy as being not the English but violence itself. When people say that he was nonviolent, that is because he was in a struggle against violence. To fight violence, you have to fight against your own desires, your own escalation to extremes against the adversary who is attacking you, and thus you have to go through an initiatory process that makes you renounce violent reciprocity. When an Englishman gave one of Gandhi's Hindu disciples a blow to the head, the Hindu fell to the ground but didn't respond to the blow. That is what shook the English, because they wondered: "How is it that we hit them, they fall, and they don't retaliate?" This ended up making them think twice, because they said to themselves: "Something's going on here, this is not possible." Gandhi won because little by little his message was heard in Britain. When he went to Britain he was welcomed as a hero. Why do we keep hammering away at him, people wondered? He's wearing a bathing suit, all he's got is a loincloth!

Very few politicians have engaged in profound reflection about psycho-politics. Gandhi said: "Listen, if you respond to violence with violence, on the individual as well as on the collective level, there is absolutely no way that you can avoid being sucked into the spiral of reciprocal violence, mimetic violence. And so you're headed for violent escalation and for a fight on the individual level." You get caught up in competitive emotions on the interdividual level and you are headed for what Girard, citing Clausewitz, calls the "escalation to extremes" on the national level. But if you quite deliberately do not respond to violence with more violence but rather accept it, then you create in your aggressors a state of surprise that is a slight modification of their state of consciousness. That is to say that the aggressor doesn't understand what is happening: "I hit him, but he didn't strike back." Thus you prepare the way for your adversary's conversion. You prepare the way for the *metanoia,* a radical change in perspective. This is exactly what Christ suggested when he said: "If someone hits you on the right cheek, turn the left cheek." Everyone thought that he was a cretin who wanted to get beaten up and that he was masochistic. This is untrue, first because by turning the other cheek you give your aggressor another view, you suggest in a way that there is a change in interlocutors, and second because Christ meant: If you respond by hitting him back on the right cheek, he will punch you, you will punch him back, there will be an escalation, a fight to the death. And if this takes place on the national level, there will be an escalation to extremes and then war. But if on the contrary you refuse to retaliate, and you look at him, there is of course the risk that he will keep beating you up, because he is carried away by his fury. But at some moment he may ask himself the following question: "How is this possible?" And that question will prepare the way for his *metanoia.* And that's what happened with the English. They wondered: "How is this possible? They come toward us, toward the soldiers, these masses of Hindus, we hit them in the face, they fall down on the ground covered in blood and they don't get up, they go away, they get back into ranks and keep calm." It made them question themselves. They wondered: *Are we doing the right thing?*

TCM: That is also what happened in the United States during the civil rights movement. Martin Luther King learned from Gandhi.

JMO: Martin Luther King did exactly the same thing. Unlike the Black Panthers, he said: "No, if we fight violence with violence, we are going to find ourselves in a cycle of revenge and then violence will take control, and we will no longer be in control of anything." This implies a kind of self-control that is consistent with the fundamental idea that we have tried to develop, namely that everyone must be called upon to transform themselves. Not only Christ but also Gandhi and Martin Luther King called upon each of us to do the considerable work of self-transformation necessary for conversion, which consists in not hitting back. Each of their undertakings was developed and had quite an important following. Even if Martin Luther King was assassinated and Christ crucified. As for Gandhi, he, too, was the victim: when the Hindus and the Muslims started to massacre each other, Gandhi fasted. Not only did he not incite the Hindus to violence, not only did he not incite them to nonviolence, but he said to them: "Look at the way you are hurting me. You are trying to attack the Muslims but instead you are hurting me, your spiritual leader. I can't stand violence and so I am going to stop eating and I am going to die!" He designated himself as the scapegoat of the violence triggered by his own supporters. And that's what stopped the violence. As soon as it was made known that Gandhi was on the brink of death and that he was in a coma, the violence in India, which involved hundreds of millions of people, stopped. And both Hindus and Muslims had their ears glued to the radio to find out whether or not Gandhi had eaten his soup.

To these examples must of course be added Nelson Mandela, who, upon being released from prison, refused to take his revenge on the whites. And who said: "No, we must not be hungry for vengeance, we must purify ourselves of our own violence, we must not become resentful, we must overcome our rivalrous urges." He set up a republic that today is sliding ineluctably, by sheer magnitude of numbers, toward the oppression of the whites and domination by the blacks, but that was not his initial idea. He was a terrorist when he was locked up, but, twenty-seven years later, he was a new man. He had become a sage, and he preached peace, nonviolence, unity, understanding between whites and blacks. He had applied to himself what he advised others to do. He was an example of what can be accomplished when we renounce violence and vengeance, and seek on the contrary to extend an olive branch to yesterday's enemies.

Here we have a few examples of people who were successful in politics, who successfully applied the method we are speaking about; that is to say that these are examples of great politicians who designated a precise, identifiable, known adversary, but one that is very hard to defeat: oneself. And they set an example by first transforming themselves, by achieving this victory over themselves, by overcoming their resentment and their rivalrous urges. And they did all this under extraordinary, and extraordinarily difficult, circumstances; not only did they have to win a victory over themselves, defeat their rivalrous urges, but they also had to avoid giving in to the passions of their followers, to the mimetic enticement of the masses who were crying out for vengeance and wanted to do battle.

They are great politicians for two essential reasons:

1. They designated a precise enemy and set an example by showing that this enemy could be defeated. In this way, they obeyed Carl Schmitt's definition of the essence of politics.
2. But they also showed their people the way to a new and more accurate vision of reality. In this, they are rare and true leaders who guide their people, who lead them and do not let themselves be led by them. One would have to go all the way back to Moses to meet with such political strength, which verges on the supernatural.

TCM: In your opinion, are there other examples of that kind in our history?

JMO: I can't think of any of that kind or on that level. There are, however, politicians who displayed two qualities that in my eyes are remarkable ones:

1. They preferred peace to war and achieved peace.
2. They made their weakness into a strength by perfecting psychopolitical technique to the utmost degree, that is to say by possessing a profound knowledge of human nature and human situations and by looking reality in the face, which, as Machiavelli said, means excluding all value judgments and all moral assessments.

The first example that comes to mind is Louis XI. He put an end to the Hundred Years' War, which had in fact been going on for three hundred years, by paying for the departure of Edward IV, the king of England. The sum was huge, but Louis XI calculated that it was the same as financing the war for a year. Moreover, this arrangement was not honorable in the chivalrous sense of the word, but Louis XI was looking for results, which is another fundamental virtue in a politician, as we said: one must define the goal and accept all the conditions necessary for its achievement.

The second example is that of Cardinal Mazarin, who came to France as an Italian. He first brought himself to the attention of both the French and the Italians because he brandished a peace treaty between the two armies that were marching toward each other at Casal. He was on horseback with the peace treaty in his hand shouting: "It's peace!" And he stopped the battle. He was then named by Louis XIII as the godfather to the future king of France, Louis XIV. He and the little one made it through the entire Fronde together and Mazarin defused violence on a daily basis by refusing to retaliate. He was a politician through and through. He took advantage of his weakness by making use of the political ruse that consists in turning the strong against one another so as to gain something from their quarrels. This is what I would call "the theory of indirect effects." But here, too, this technique is based on the two very important pillars that we already pointed out:

1. Perfect knowledge of the various political players and of the hidden motives that make them act. In other words, the ability to see reality and an intuitive grasp of mimetic psychology, which includes being clear-sighted about oneself and the capacity for controlling one's own rivalrous urges.
2. The precise and realistic designation of the intended goal, which takes precedence over everything and which must never be lost to sight. Any concession was possible, save for the one that could interfere with the goal to be achieved.

Mazarin's only protection was his clerical garments. The nobility was always hesitant to assassinate Mazarin "officially." In his presence, no noble would have dared to run him through with his sword because they said to themselves, "He is a cardinal of the Roman Catholic Church after all, we are Christians, and we could be excommunicated by the pope or, worse still, damned. We can't kill him like that." Armed with this sole weapon and with the legitimacy that the queen regent's protection conferred upon him, he managed little by little to disarm the nobility and the parliament and to transmit to his godson Louis XIV an intact royal authority.

Mazarin had yet another political quality of the first order: he wanted peace. His ultimate objective was to establish a lasting peace in Europe, based on peace with Spain. To this end, his political wisdom led him to avoid humiliating his enemies or making reckless use of his strength: first he stopped the advance of Turenne's armies, which had been victorious beyond the Rhine, so as to save the adversary's face and avoid destabilizing the states that then made up Germany. He stopped Turenne, who had vanquished the Spanish, for a second time, preventing him from conquering Brussels and the Netherlands, once more for the same reasons and because crushing and humiliating the adversary would not serve the ends of peace, the political goal that he had set for himself.

This example leads me to think that the old adage: *Si vis pacem, para bellum* should be replaced by *Si vis bellum, para pacem*.

I will add the following: it was often said at the time and it is still said that Mazarin had influence over the queen regent, Ann of Austria, because he was her lover. What crude psychology! Mazarin would never have committed such a grievous psychopolitical error: he was a confidant, a friend, a humble servant, a minister, weak, alone, depending for his protection solely on the queen, who could not do without him and who took him completely into her confidence because she felt that she could control him. Had he become her lover, he would have found himself ensnarled in an inextricable series of complications, quarrels, reconciliations, and jealous flare-ups, and he would have wasted all of his energy managing their love affair, with all of the difficulties and traps accompanying a mimetic rivalry that would have gnawed away at their relationship. With respect to the queen, the attitude he adopted consisted in always maintaining a "one-down" position, as transactional analysts would say, and this was what ensured his survival and proved his psychopolitical mastery.

In studying world history, we could surely find other examples of shrewd, remarkable politicians. For example, Marguerite Yourcenar portrays the emperor Hadrian as a sage, a politician, and at the same time a philosopher in search of the real: "Let us try, if we can, to enter into death with open eyes,"[73] such are the emperor's last words and the book's last sentence.

Louis XI, Mazarin, Hadrian, but also Gandhi, Martin Luther King, Nelson Mandela, the Dalai Lama, and Pope John Paul II each provide us with examples of politicians whose common trait was to have overcome their own passions before inviting their followers to do the same.

Corneille sums this up admirably in his play *Cinna* (act 5), when he has the emperor Augustus say: "Je suis maître de moi comme de l'univers." "I am master of myself as I am of the universe." This should be read in the same way as the phrase: "Forgive us our trespasses as we forgive those who have trespassed against us." The adverb "as" thus indicates a causal relationship. We should understand: "I am master of the universe because—and insofar as—I am master of myself." Being the master of oneself means not being the plaything of one's desire, not being deluded, not being the puppet of mimetic rivalries.

TCM: The examples you give are enlightening but quite few in number. This is hardly cause for optimism. In your opinion, what is the psychopolitical situation today? What are the most urgent problems that must be addressed?

JMO: It seems to me that there are currently three types of problems that demand urgent political attention and reflection:

1. The Problem of Fear

On a practical level, experience and history teach us that the only effective brake—though even this effectiveness was limited—that there was against violence was the fear of vengeance, that is to say fear of retaliation from the enemy clan or fear of justice.

The problem of the death penalty has been debated and put to rest in our European democracies, but in many countries it is still far from being resolved. But that is not what concerns me here. What the entire world urgently needs is a new form of awareness capable of putting a stop to violence by means other than fear.

What is unfortunate today is that the great powers want to wage "zero casualty" wars so as to satisfy public opinion. But it is zero casualties on the American side, for example, that counts. The number of Iraqi, Afghan, or other deaths is without importance.

The excessive use of violence against an infinitely less well-armed enemy is toxic for the aggressor. It is true that the pilot who drops his smart bomb five miles from his target without seeing any of the effects it is going to bring about feels totally invincible and sheltered from punishment, but the images of destruction, of the dead and the wounded, transmitted by every television station, end up making the "victors'" experience negative and degrading feelings about themselves.

Psychopolitics must condemn this excessive use of power and strength and strive to replace fear with wisdom so as to put a stop to its own violence, all the more so because it is becoming clear that this devastating power achieves no concrete results, apart from embedding a tenacious resentment and a rancorous hatred in the hearts of the defeated populations and serving as a justification and driving force of terrorism.

Today, psychopolitics must not only impose limits on its own strength but also address the second problem of modern conflicts.

2. The Problem of "Saving Face"

If you want to achieve peace and a lasting and real peace, it is imperative to enable the enemy to save face. That is what Mazarin sought to do, that is what MacArthur did in Japan, and that is what Marshall did in Europe. The problem is fundamentally the same in both politics and psychology.

In fact, it is impossible to make peace without saving the adversary's face. But for this to happen an important condition must be fulfilled: it is the strongest side that must enable the weaker side to save face.

The first example that comes to mind is Henri IV, King of France, after his conversion to Catholicism, who, in the stronger position, "declared peace" to the Protestants by issuing the Edict of Nantes, healing the scars left by the Saint Bartholomew's Day massacre.

The second example is General de Gaulle, the hero of World War II, president of the French Republic, who, during the Algerian War, enabled the Fellagha, until then labeled as criminals, rebels, and terrorists, to save face by offering them "the peace of the valiant." It was by recognizing their dignity and showing respect for their cause that he was able to bring them to the negotiating table. In saying what he did, General de Gaulle raised them up, because he was in the position of strength. When the weaker of the two parties takes the initiative, this approach is ineffective. Almost twenty years later, on the floor of the UN, Yasser Arafat offered "the peace of the valiant" to the Israelis. The only response to his proposition was a scornful burst of laughter—he was the weaker party.

This is equally true on the psychological level. In principle, it is the parents who must forgive their children and not the other way around. I will also tell you the story of a woman who came for a consultation saying that she was going to ask for a divorce because her husband had cheated on her. I asked to see the husband, who sheepishly admitted that he had gotten carried away and embarked on an affair with his secretary, and who said to me: "How can I redeem myself?" "You can't," I told him. "Let me see your wife again."

Seeing his spouse once more, I said to her: "Madame, in this situation, you are in the position of strength. Your husband did something dumb and he knows it. You are the only one who can save the situation by giving him back his dignity and ceasing to condemn him. You must forgive him and above all you must forgive yourself for having failed to avoid or been unable to avoid what happened. Because you are the stronger of the two, because you are in the right, and because he is in the wrong. Whether you want to save the marriage or not is up to you, but in either case, be sure you are making a fully informed choice."

Over the course of my forty years as a psychiatrist, whenever someone comes into my office I have looked for a solution, the solution to his or her specific problem. Some people are further along than others. The journey may be the same for everyone, but each of us is at a different stage of that journey. And so you have to see where the patient is, take them by the hand,

and help them take a few steps in the right direction. And in psychopolitics, this applies not only to each and every individual, but also to big groups, big communities, in other words to nations. Because I think that fundamentally, individuals react to one another in exactly the same way as nations do. There is no essential difference, merely a difference of degree. And in the end, what we have to find are original ways of helping people pull through. What do I mean by original ways? In "individual" psychopolitics, you have to find a way of allowing the person to let go of his or her symptom without losing face. In the same way, in international affairs, you have to find a way of enabling the adversary to give up some of his demands without losing face. I believe that the notion of "saving face" is of fundamental importance, both in individual and collective psychology. If a patient has been unable to walk for years and the whole family is organized around this phenomenon, a special car has been purchased, and the patient is wheeled around by the whole family, I cannot come and tell this patient abruptly to abandon his symptom and get up and walk because then he would lose face and would look like he had been fooling everybody on purpose.

In the same way, at the international level, if a nation lays claim to a territory or to some advantage or whatever, and if you want to make that nation give up the claim, you have to enable it to save face. So seeking a way of saving face is, in my opinion, one of the fundamental elements of psychopolitics.

TCM: We are dealing with leaders who are extremely proud people and who want above all for people to look on them with admiration, and who precisely are afraid of losing face.

JMO: What characterizes the failure of politics is that leaders seek to solve problems without enabling their adversaries to save face. The greatest political wisdom and the greatest political art, which in a way is what gives politics its legitimacy, is precisely enabling your adversaries to save face each and every time. I am reminded in particular of a leader whom I knew well and who was the president of his country. There was a kind of revolt, almost a revolution, in his country, and all of the clan heads and feudal chiefs were gathered around him. And they couldn't manage to reach an agreement. And this politician used a bit of humor to save the day. He said: "You're all chiefs, but believe me, a chief of staff is better than a staff of chiefs." This way of doing things takes the drama out of the conflict or demand.

3. THE PROBLEM OF HOPELESSNESS

There is a third aspect of psychopolitics that is just as applicable to psychological cases as it is to political cases or nations: giving people *hope*. The person who comes into my psychiatrist's office must leave with a glimmer of hope, saying to him or herself: "Maybe there is a solution that will enable me to take care of my problem, and not only my problem but also the problem I have with my partner, with my parents, my friends, my coworkers, my secretary, my boss, and so on." You must give people hope.

Today we are embroiled in a crisis. One of the essences of politics must be giving hope to the masses, to the people. The whole world said: "Everything is going to change, there is a glimmer of hope because Obama was elected." The Nobel Prize consecrated this hope and made it official, whereas in reality it is purely subjective. There is something about politics that has always been quasi-sacred, quasi-divine, in the sense that what it gives, what it offers, is not completely material. It's always something quasi-miraculous, something without much material substance. Obama didn't come along and say: "Okay, so I figured it out, from now on each one of you is going to get a thousand dollars a month." But he gave a kind of hope to the whole of humanity. There is something completely immaterial and, I would say, almost spiritual about this phenomenon. It is in this sense that politics is related to the sacred, that it has roots in the sacred and the miraculous. This is what gives politics its grandeur. And this is equally true for the psychiatrist who must give hope to the patient who has come for a consultation and who is by definition in despair. During his campaign and during the first weeks of his presidency, Obama was able to create this "state of grace," but I am willing to bet that when he gets into the nuts and bolts of administrative and technical decisions, his popularity will diminish.

Another political virtue consists in appearing able to gather people together. Every time a politician succeeds in gaining power, even without going through the democratic process, he does so by gathering people. For example, Mitterand managed to get elected twice by stressing his capacity for gathering, using calming, confidence-building slogans: *la force tranquille,* "calm strength." This slogan says: "Come to me, everyone, I'm nobody's enemy. I'm strong, but I'm not aggressive." Meanwhile, in 2002, Jacques Chirac was elected with an 80 percent majority because he gathered all of France together against a wonderfully targeted scapegoat, Jean-Marie Le Pen. So there is a capacity for gathering people that plays a fundamental role in politics.

This capacity for gathering amounts to saying: "We're all on the same team. Anyone who wants to come is welcome. I'm not partisan." There is a kind of gravitational pull toward nonrivalry. This is what gathering people together is all about. And I think this is pretty much what Obama did. You want me to be black? I'm black. You want me to be white? I'm white, too. You want me to be Muslim? Well, I'm also a little Muslim. You want me to be Christian? I go to church. I'm young, but I'm also old. I have a little gray hair. Everyone can find what he or she is looking for.

When French president Nicolas Sarkozy included members of the opposition in his cabinet, I think that he was also trying to gather people in this way.

Finally, I would like to come back for a moment to the problem of fear, which appears to me to be central. Krishnamurti writes: "we are afraid of the known and afraid of the unknown . . . let us ask ourselves, can this society, based on competition, brutality and fear, come to an end?"[74] Further on, he adds: "As long as we are frightened by life, we shall be frightened by death."[75]

What is weakening the Western, developed countries is fear, that is to say that we refuse to take the slightest risk and are becoming security fanatics: social security, job security, financial security, highway safety, bodily safety; the imperative to stay in good health, to be vigilant about sanitation, to avoid suffering, to prevent aging, to control life (birth control) and to control death (euthanasia).

We want a life that is risk-free. Yet life is a risk. Is the "risk-free" life that we want the same as the life lived by people in Asia, Africa, and South America?

Echoing Krishnamurti, Jean Paul II was speaking above all to us, I think, with his famous words: "Be not afraid!" We must listen to both of these great sages, and politics must draw inspiration from them when looking for ways of fighting terrorism. The problem can be stated as follows: How can people who are afraid of life avoid being terrorized by people who are unafraid of death?

TCM: You have just defined the practical steps that politics must take at the present time so as not to fail—in other words, if I have understood you correctly, so as not to get bogged down in wars that go on and on forever and to make sure that people do not become disenchanted.

I would now like to bring up a subject that is a bit more precise but that surely overlaps with what you have been saying. In a recent text, you write: "In our culture, the rites of passage that ensured that order and peace would be maintained were embodied by school, mandatory military service, church, boy scouts, etc. These rites have more or less disappeared."[76]

JMO: The purpose of initiatory rites is to enable each of us to live through the experience of death. Giving everyone the experience of death leads to a kind of wisdom. When you know what death is, you won't take lives. Everyone who goes through the initiatory process, having experienced death and resurrection, knows what life is worth. This converts people to a nonviolent attitude and leads them to avoid violence, because they know the damage that violence can do not only to others but also to themselves. I think that Christ's experience gives us the experience of the true, "factual" resurrection. Gandhi, for his part, suffered agonies: "Listen to me! I am going to die if you don't stop killing one another. You are killing me." It was a rough outline of the Passion. The resurrection came both when Gandhi came out of his coma and when India emerged from chaos.

It's difficult to invent new rites of passage when the old ones have been eliminated. Nonetheless, institutions, groups, communities, and even churches must be encouraged to be innovative in the way they deal with young people, to give young people an initiatory experience. In any event, young people will invent substitute rites of passage in the form of drug addictions, violent, suicidal behavior, juvenile delinquency, and so forth. I addressed this tendency in my 1973 book *La Personne du toxicomane.*[77]

TCM: This is proof *a contrario* that people cannot do without rites.

JMO: If we don't provide positive rites that lead people toward life and guide them in life, they will invent negative ones that lead them toward death.

CHAPTER EIGHT

In Conclusion.

TCM: As we bring our conversations to a close, what advice might we give to people bearing political, religious, and psychotherapeutic responsibilities?

JMO: I doubt that anyone is asking us for advice. However, perhaps they could derive some small benefit from reading this little book, or in any case the works listed in the bibliography.

TCM: In the final part of his book, Sloterdijk gives some advice that he addresses to the French and the Germans in particular, but also to the rest of the world in a more general way. He writes that reconciliation should ultimately lead to "mutual disinterest and defascination. . . . Only after detachment from one another has occurred can the good and useful things, which we describe with such contemporary cardinal words as cooperation and integration, start to gain momentum. If Germans and Europeans have any advice for the rest of the world, especially for those contemporary areas of conflict where the duellists are hot with fascination for each other, such as India and Pakistan, Israel and its neighbors, the Islamists and the Occidentalists, and possibly also the USA and China—then it might well sound like this. 'Do it the same way we did, don't be too interested in each other!'"[78]

I fear that the "mutual disinterest" that Sloterdijk recommends may be dangerous, for throughout humanity's history reciprocity has always been conflictual.

JMO: What you have just said is proof that you are a devoutly orthodox Girardian, and naturally I approve, since René Girard has taught us that any sort of reciprocity is potentially rivalrous and conflictual.

But as far as this piece of advice from Sloterdijk is concerned, I would add that to me it appears depressingly reductive. It would lead to creating a world in which everyone would be ignorant of and indifferent to his neighbors. In any event, it would be difficult to bring such a world into existence given that we are living in an era of globalization, in which North Korea need only wiggle its little finger to plunge the whole world into a state of extreme agitation. In their book *Le monde d'après,* Matthieu Pigasse and Gilles Finchelstein, having pointed out the risks of too much state control, add: "The second risk is withdrawing in on oneself, isolationism. Nationalist withdrawal. Protectionist withdrawal. Populist withdrawal. The kinds of withdrawal may vary, but the result will always be a tragic one."[79]

TCM: So we must maintain a good balance between fascination and indifference. But practically speaking, how do we do that?

JMO: There is of course no simple, definitive answer to these eternal questions.

It seems to me, however, that the time has come for religion, politics, and psychology to face up to the fact that the mechanisms that have driven them for centuries are obsolete:

- Religion must take note of the fact that the revelation supplied by the Passion and made explicit in René Girard's work has put us in an apocalyptic situation. In other words, we are no longer protected by the sacred, and so this is no longer the time for pointing fingers, for looking for the guilty party, for stigmatizing evil, for fanaticism and claims of supremacy. We are in trouble, and we have to make a drastic decision between humility and reconciliation or universal destruction.
- Politics must take note of the fact that its essence is also its duty: designating the enemy. When it designates terrorism, global warming, poverty, hunger, and so on, it must understand that what it is designating are not enemies but dangers. Scientists and researchers in all disciplines must be roused into action to try to find solutions to these problems. But politics

must, in my opinion, clearly designate a precise, known, clearly designated enemy that is obvious to each of us and that underlies all of these
problems: ourselves. The greatest sages, wise men, and philosophers have
all said something similar, each in their own way, and we have given
some examples. This is not a utopia. This is reality and it is unavoidable;
we must force ourselves to accept it if we want to avoid the end of the
world.

- Finally, psychology and psychopathology must stop looking for an intra-
  or extrapsychic responsible party at the root of our fears, our anxieties,
  our despair, our depression, and our violence. They must acknowledge at
  their particular level what religion and politics must acknowledge at the
  public level: the only thing that makes hope, repose, calm, and happiness
  possible is managing our relationships with others in a nonconflictual
  way, and all our pathologies are first and foremost relational pathologies.
  Krishnamurti writes: "There is only you—your relationship with others
  and with the world—there is nothing else."[80]

Politics, religion, and psychology must all—each at its own level—recognize the vital necessity of "freeing oneself from the known," as Krishnamurti
would say, and make the considerable effort required to discover the real,
reality as it is, whether it is pleasant or not, to give up illusion, the mad desire
that mistakes desire for reality. All three must give up the elementary mechanism that characterizes both human nature and culture: *expulsion.*

- From the dawn of humanity, medicine has sought cures in expulsion: for
  centuries, the only treatments were enemas, purgatives, herbal laxatives,
  bloodlettings, and so forth.
- Psychology and psychopathology, as we have said, also had recourse
  to expulsion: sperm and menses drainage, exorcism and the purifying
  expulsion of demons. Later on, the expulsion of traumatic unconscious
  memories through cathartic talking cures.
- Finally, politics, by designating the enemy, expels it from the national
  community and condemns it to death. This is true of both the foreign
  enemy, who comes from the exterior, and the interior enemy. And in
  politics, too, expulsion is not always lethal and death can be replaced by
  exile, the most illustrious example of this being Napoleon's exile, first
  on Elba, from which he returned, and then much farther away, on Saint
  Helena, where he remained until his death. The expulsion of Louis XVI
  was more radical.

The great thinkers and sages can help us in our efforts to renounce the universal, ubiquitous, and all-too-human mechanism of expulsion, on condition that we lend our ears to what they have said and that we take them seriously. Kant, for example, encourages us to take charge of our own lives: "Have the courage to use your own understanding."[81]

For Spinoza, human life can be defined by the striving toward peace of mind and freedom from the passions, what he calls "blessedness" (*beatitudo*).[82] This goal determines the effectiveness of the means—understanding and self-mastery—put to work in the quest to "Know thyself." And Spinoza gives some advice as he embarks on this enterprise: *Caute,* which is to say, "Be careful," "Proceed with caution." This is the same recommendation that is to be found in many rites of initiation when the neophyte is handed over to the care of those who are going to make him undergo the ordeals of his initiation: "Be careful, guide him, and bring him back safe and sound."

Spinoza invites each of us to aim for freedom, peace of mind, and happiness. Yet at the end of the *Ethics* he cautions that "all things excellent are as difficult as they are rare."[83] Freedom is not a given, a gift-wrapped present that man receives at birth. Freedom is a continuous process, a gradual and boundless liberation through constant effort, and freedom is in reality a ceaseless, initiatory struggle against oneself, against the mimetic mechanisms that make us their plaything, of which we are the complacent, consenting, and quite often fanatical puppets and marionettes.

What are we struggling against? I have said and written it many times. I'll sum it up here: man and woman left the Garden of Eden and entered the world where we live through the play of desire, and desire is mimetic.

Desire is the fundamental principle underlying everything and that is why it must be understood. Philippe Danino writes of Spinoza's thought on this point: "To the extent that the *conatus* is the essence of everything, desire, which is one of its manifestations, would be unable to give man a specific place in nature. . . . We are desire not because we constitute an exception in nature, but to the contrary because we are fully a part and take part in the infinite dynamic of nature."[84] Further on, he adds a clarification that makes Spinoza into a precursor of the mimetic theory: "It is not necessary to be lacking in anything to experience desire. . . . The greedy person does not need to be lacking money in order to want more."[85]

This passage opens up a clear distinction between desire, on the one hand, and need or lack on the other. It makes desire the fundamental driving force of psychology. In *Ethics* III, proposition 9, cited by Philippe Danino, Spinoza states: "it is clear that we neither strive for, nor will, neither want, nor desire anything because we judge it to be good; on the contrary, we judge something to be good because we strive for it, will it, want it, and desire it."[86]

And why do we desire something that is not intrinsically good in itself? Because it has been pointed out to us by someone else, by our model, whom René Girard calls the mediator—and we arrive quite naturally at the mimetic theory. Spinoza writes: the "imitation of the affects" when "related to desire" is "called *emulation,* which, therefore, is nothing but *the desire for a thing which is generated in us from the fact that we imagine others like us to have the same desire.*"[87] And he adds: "envy is generally joined to this affect."[88] In proposition 32, he goes even further toward describing mimetic desire: "From the mere fact that we imagine someone to enjoy something . . . we shall love that thing and desire to enjoy it. But we imagine his enjoyment of this thing as an obstacle to our joy. Therefore we shall strive that he not possess it."[89]

What follows is even more striking from the point of view that concerns us here: "human nature is so constituted that men pity the unfortunate and envy the fortunate, and [envy them] with greater hate the more they love the thing they imagine the other to possess. We see, then, that from the same property of human nature from which it follows that men are compassionate, it also follows that the same men are envious and ambitious . . . children, because their bodies are continually, as it were, in a state of equilibrium, laugh or cry simply because they see others laugh or cry. Moreover, whatever they see others do, they immediately desire to imitate it. And finally, they desire for themselves all those things by which they imagine others are pleased—because, as we have said, the images of things are the very affections of the human body, or modes by which the human body is affected by external causes, and disposed to do this or that."[90]

We desire because the other desires. The model draws us toward the things he himself desires, the mere fact of his possessing them making it obvious that he desires them and therefore that they are desirable. This mechanism is what makes any kind of learning possible: through imitation and repetition the child gradually acquires his parents' language and little by little their entire culture. Later, he will learn everything he knows how to do by copying his teachers and by reproducing what they show him. In every learning process, mimetic desire is positive and constructive because the model remains a model and the pupil copies not only the model's gesture—the gesture of a teacher who is showing how to write, for example—but also the model's desire, since the teacher desires that the pupil learn how to write. The pupil loves the teacher who teaches well and the teacher loves the pupil who learns well.

Later, and by means of the same mimetic mechanism, desire will bear on objects that belong to the model but that the model does not want to give up. The model may then become a rival or an obstacle and the disciple may nourish feelings of resentment and hatred toward the model and seek to acquire the model-rival's object by force or violence.

It is the transfiguration of the model into a rival or an obstacle that generates violence, that creates all the misfortune in the world, and that prevents men and women from being free. As soon as they get caught up in a rivalrous passion, human beings lose their freedom and their clear-sightedness, and on the political level, as soon as nations get caught up in this mechanism, they "escalate to extremes" and there is nothing that can stop this uncontrollable process.

Finally, absolute rivalrous passion is revealed in the religious fanaticism that deifies rivalrous desire and makes it into the Good for which it fights against the deified desire of its (Evil) enemies.

To say that politics must designate the enemy as being ourselves and that it must draw religion and psychology along in its wake is to say that politics—with leaders setting the example at first, and then through all kinds of practical measures—must encourage human beings to free themselves from their own violence by retransforming their rivals and their obstacles into models, in other words by following the road to freedom thus created.

TCM: If I understand you correctly, working to transform oneself means changing one's perspective, radically altering the way we see our enemies.

JMO: As long as we have not changed ourselves and "seen" the real, we are a danger to ourselves and to others. We are "sleepwalkers," as Arthur Koestler says, "asleep," as Gurdjieff says, prisoners of an individual and collective mimetic phenomenon that is sometimes called hypnosis; we do not know what we are doing.

There is an urgent need for us to *wake up* and *see* the real.

TCM: What is your conclusion?

JMO: At the end of his earthly voyage among human beings, Christ, dying on the cross, sums up all of human functioning for his Father in an admirable phrase: "They know not what they do!"

It seems to me that the very best thing that politics could do today is encourage people to see the reality of what they are, the mimetic relationships that unify and divide them but that they totally fail to recognize and understand, and to give them a clearly identified enemy—themselves—and a precise objective: freeing themselves from their passions, their rivalries, their violence, and from all the mimetic mechanisms that make puppets out of them.

In my opinion, psychopolitics, illuminated my mimetic psychology, has an important role to play in this undertaking.

TCM: Do you think there's any chance that politicians will get involved in this undertaking, that they will become conscious of the danger that is lying in wait and give up the old sacrificial recipe?

JMO: If you had asked me the same question a few days ago, I would have been pessimistic. But in reading today's newspaper, I see that at the Oxford meeting of TED Global, the European version of the prestigious TED Conference (for Technology, Entertainment, and Design), Prime Minister Gordon Brown, showing images of Hiroshima and Biafra, "called for the emergence of a global collective consciousness founded on an ethics of responsibility, the only thing capable of curing the ills of our world."[91]

In such statements, I see a light at the end of the tunnel. An important politician is calling for all of us to raise our awareness and to take responsibility. This is perfectly in line with the direction in which these conversations have taken us.

Notes

1. *Translator's note:* The French language has two words for politics: *la politique,* which takes the feminine article and corresponds roughly to what we think of in English when we talk about "politics," and *le politique,* which is masculine and refers to a more conceptual, archaic notion of politics—the essence of politics, the political domain. After consultation with the author, I have translated this more conceptual word—the one that Jean-Michel Oughourlian prefers to use when talking about political matters—variously as "the political mechanism," "the political power," or simply as "politics," depending on the context and the shades of meaning implied.

2. Institute for Conflict Research.

3. Miles Copeland, *The Game of Nations: The Amorality of Power Politics* (New York: Simon and Schuster, 1970).

4. Sun-Tzu, *The Art of War,* tr. John Minford (New York: Penguin Classics, 2005), 17.

5. Josy Eisenberg, *Dieu et les juifs* (Paris: Albin Michel, 2009), 68.

6. Sun-Tzu, *The Art of War,* 4–6.

7. The French public greatly appreciates imitators and impersonators, who are national celebrities and are capable of filling up an entire stadium when they perform.

8. Jean-Michel Oughourlian, *The Genesis of Desire,* tr. Eugene Webb (East Lansing: Michigan State University Press, 2010). See chapter 3, part 2: "The Discovery of Mirror Neurons."

9. Friedrich Hacker, *Terreur et terrorisme* (Paris: Flammarion, 1976), 134. An English version exists (Frederick J. Hacker, *Crusaders, Criminals, Crazies: Terror and Terrorism in Our Time* [New York: W. W. Norton, 1976]) but as it differs from the French edition in many respects it was decided to translate directly from the former.

10. David Galula, *Counterinsurgency Warfare: Theory and Practice* (New York, London: Frederick A. Praeger, 1964), x.

11. Pierre Corneille, *Le Cid*, tr. Richard Wilbur (Boston: Houghton Mifflin Harcourt, 2009), act II, scene 2, p. 38.

12. Corneille, *Le Cid*, act 2, scene 1, p. 34.

13. Fabrice d'Almeida, "La joie. L'été de 1914," *Marianne*, issue 641, August 1, 2009, http://www.marianne2.fr/La-joie-L-ete-1914_a185331.html (6/10/2011).

14. d'Almeida, "La joie."

15. Philippe Bouvard, "Mourez ! La télé mettra les petits cercueils dans les grands . . ." *Le Figaro Magazine*, issue 122, September 12, 2009, http://www.lefigaro.fr/lefigaromagazine/2009/09/12/01006–20090912ARTFIG00078—mourez-la-tele-mettra-les-petits-cercueils-dans-les-grands-.php (6/6/2011).

16. René Girard, *Battling to the End: Conversations with Benoît Chantre*, tr. Mary Baker (East Lansing: Michigan State University Press, 2010), 139.

17. Galula, *Counterinsurgency Warfare*, xii.

18. Galula, *Counterinsurgency Warfare*, 53–54.

19. Galula, *Counterinsurgency Warfare*, 7. Emphasis added.

20. Hacker, *Terreur et terrorisme*, 21.

21. Niccolò Machiavelli, *The Prince*, tr. George Bull (London: Penguin Classics, 2003), 8.

22. Machiavelli, *The Prince*, 9.

23. Galula, *Counterinsurgency Warfare*, xi.

24. Galula, *Counterinsurgency Warfare*, 11.

25. Guy Sorman, "Mourir pour Kaboul?" *Le Futur c'est tout de suite*, August 12, 2009, http://gsorman.typepad.com/guy_sorman/2009/08/mourir-pour-kaboul-1.html (6/6/2011).

26. "When the economic markets are globalized, differences are erased, and everyone becomes the rival of everyone else. What the state is weakened, the possibility of channeling and mastering violence disappears. Local conflicts multiply, people cling to their communitarian identities, there are clashes of ambition, and lives no longer have any value. The disappearance of the Soviet Union caused one of the world's policemen to disappear. The future failure of the hyperempire, the sophistication of weapons, and the multiplication of actors could even, by converging, generate, within the hyperempire, a global conflict, a planetary uprising, a *hyperconflict* much more destructive than any local or world conflict that came before." Jacques Attali, *Une brève histoire de l'avenir* (Paris: Fayard, 2006).

27. Carl Schmitt, *The Concept of the Political*, tr. George Schwab (Chicago: University of Chicago Press, 2007), 65.

28. Schmitt, *Concept of the Political,* 26.

29. Schmitt, *Concept of the Political,* 47.

30. Cf. p. 44 of the French edition, *La Notion de politique* (Paris: Flammarion, 1992). This preface is not included in the English translation.

31. Schmitt, *Concept of the Political*, 28.

32. Schmitt, *Concept of the Political*, 29.

33. Schmitt, *Concept of the Political*, 29.

34. Schmitt, *Concept of the Political*, 30–31.

35. Schmitt, *Concept of the Political*, 33.

36. Schmitt, *Concept of the Political*, 33.

37. Schmitt, *Concept of the Political*, 34.

38. Sigmund Freud, *Group Psychology and the Analysis of the Ego*, tr. James Strachey (New York: Norton, 1959), 59.

39. René Laforgue, *Talleyrand, l'homme de la France* (Geneva: Editions du Mont Blanc, 1962), 12.

40. Peter Sloterdijk, *Theory of the Post-War Periods*, tr. Robert Payne (Vienna: Springer-Verlag, 2009), 42.

41. Sloterdijk, *Theory of Post-War Periods*, 42. The *modèle* referred to by Sloterdijk corresponds to Girard's mimetic model, while the *repoussoir* is a tool that is used for pushing something back, or figuratively speaking, something that thwarts or foils; it thus corresponds to what Girard calls the "rival" or the "obstacle."

42. Sloterdijk, *Theory of Post-War Periods*, 13–14.

43. Sloterdijk, *Theory of Post-War Periods*, 18.

44. Sloterdijk, *Theory of Post-War Periods*, 14.

45. Sloterdijk, *Theory of Post-War Periods*, 48.

46. Milan Kundera, *Immortality*, tr. Peter Kussi (New York: Grove, 1991), 113.

47. Kundera, *Immortality*, 114.

48. Kundera, *Immortality*, 114.

49. Kundera, *Immortality*, 115.

50. Kundera, *Immortality*, 115.

51. Kundera, *Immortality*, 116.

52. See, for example, the allegorical engraving "Le Diable d'argent" in P. L. Jacob, *Dix-septième siècle; lettres, sciences et arts, France, 1590–1700* (Paris: Firmin-Didot, 1882), 159.

53. Clearstream is the name of a banking organization in which some people in France pretended to have discovered the name Nicolas Sarkozy, leading contender for the presidency at the time, and therefore tried to make the French public believe that he had hidden money outside of the country.

54. Girard, *Battling to the End*, ix.

55. André Chouraqui, tr., *La Bible* (Paris: Desclée de Brouwer, 1989), 2379.

56. Girard, *Battling to the End*, x.

57. Girard, *Battling to the End*, x.

58. Hacker, *Terreur et terrorisme,* 89.

59. Girard, *Battling to the End,* xiv.

60. Girard, *Battling to the End,* xiii–xiv.

61. Emphasis added.

62. Mark 13:8, King James version.

63. Girard, *Battling to the End,* 116.

64. Girard, *Battling to the End,* 211.

65. Pierre Manent, *Les Naissances de la politique moderne* (Paris: Gallimard, 2007), 22.

66. Manent, *Naissances,* 23.

67. Machiavelli, *The Prince,* 57–58.

68. Simone Bertière, *Mazarin, le maître du jeu* (Paris: Editions de Fallois, 2007), 632.

69. Bertière, *Mazarin,* 632.

70. Corneille, *Le Cid,* act 2, scene 1, p. 44.

71. See *Parler d'amour au bout du gouffre* (Paris: Odile Jacob, 2004), 35.

72. Milan Kundera, *Slowness,* tr. Linda Asher (New York: HarperCollins, 1996), 64.

73. Marguerite Yourcenar, *The Memoirs of Hadrian,* tr. Grace Frick (New York: Farrar, Straus and Giroux, 1988), 295.

74. Jiddu Krishnamurti, *Freedom from the Known,* ed. Mary Lutyens (Southhampton: Camelot Press, 1983), 13–14.

75. Krishnamurti, *Freedom from the Known,* 77.

76. Preface to Bernard Gaillard, *Adolescents qui dérangent: Entre différenciation et provocation* (Paris: l'Harmattan, 2009), 7–10.

77. Jean-Michel Oughourlian, *La Personne du toxicomane* (Toulouse: Privat, 1978).

78. Sloterdijk, *Theory of Post-War Periods,* 49.

79. Matthieu Pigasse and Gilles Finchelstein, *Le monde d'après—une crise sans précédent* (Paris: Plon, 2009), 209.

80. Krishnamurti, *Freedom from the Known,* 15.

81. *The Philosophy of Kant,* ed. Carl J. Friedrich (New York: The Modern Library, 1949), 132.

82. See Benedict de Spinoza, *Ethics,* part V, "*Of the Power of the Intellect,* or *On Human Freedom,*" tr. Edwin Curly (London: Penguin, 1996), 160–181.

83. Benedict de Spinoza, *Ethics,* 181.

84. Philippe Danino, *Le Nouvel Observateur,* July–August 2009, special issue on Spinoza, 38.

85. Danino, *Le Nouvel Observateur,* 39.

86. Benedict de Spinoza, *Ethics,* 76.

87. Benedict de Spinoza, *Ethics,* 84.

88. Benedict de Spinoza, *Ethics*, 110.

89. Benedict de Spinoza, *Ethics*, 87.

90. Benedict de Spinoza, *Ethics*, 87.

91. Flore Vasseur, "Quand l'élite mondiale imagine l'avenir,"*Le Figaro*, August 24, 2009, http://www.lefigaro.fr/sciences/2009/08/29/01008–20090829ARTFIG00002-quand-l-elite-mondiale-imagine-l-avenir-.php (6/10/2011).

Bibliography

Attali, Jacques. *Une brève histoire de l'avenir*. Paris: Fayard, 2006.

Bertière, Simone. *Mazarin, le maître du jeu*. Paris: Editions de Fallois, 2007.

Chouraqui, André, tr. *La Bible*. Paris: Desclée de Brouwer, 1989.

Copeland, Miles. *The Game of Nations: The Amorality of Power Politics*. New York: Simon and Schuster, 1970.

Corneille, Pierre. *Le Cid*. Tr. Richard Wilbur. New York: Houghton Mifflin Harcourt, 2009.

Eisenberg, Josy. *Dieu et les juifs*. Paris: Albin Michel, 2009.

Freud, Sigmund. *Group Psychology and the Analysis of the Ego*. Tr. James Strachey. New York: Norton, 1959.

Gaillard, Bernard. *Adolescents qui dérangent: Entre différenciation et provocation*. Preface by Jean-Michel Oughourlian. Paris: l'Harmattan, 2009.

Galula, David. *Counterinsurgency Warfare: Theory and Practice*. New York: Frederick A. Praeger, 1964.

Girard, René. *Battling to the End: Conversations with Benoît Chantre*. Tr. Mary Baker. East Lansing: Michigan State University Press, 2010.

Hacker, Frederick J. *Crusaders, Criminals, Crazies: Terror and Terrorism in Our Time*. New York: Norton, 1977.

Krishnamurti, *Freedom from the Known*. Ed. Mary Lutyens. Southhampton: Camelot Press, 1983.

Kundera, Milan. *Immortality*. Tr. Peter Kussi. New York: Grove, 1991.

————. *Slowness*. Tr. Linda Asher. New York: HarperCollins, 1996.

Laforgue, René. *Talleyrand, l'homme de la France*. Geneva: Editions du Mont Blanc, 1962.

Machiavelli, Niccolò. *The Prince*. Tr. George Bull. London: Penguin Classics, 2003.

Manent, Pierre. *Les Naissances de la politique moderne*. Paris: Gallimard, 2007.

Oughourlian, Jean-Michel. *La Personne du toxicomane*. Toulouse: Privat, 1978.

————. *The Genesis of Desire*. Tr. Eugene Webb. East Lansing: Michigan State University Press, 2010.

Pigasse, Matthieu, and Gilles Finchelstein. *Le monde d'après—une crise sans précédent*. Paris: Plon, 2009.

Schmitt, Carl. *The Concept of the Political*. Tr. George Schwab. Chicago: University of Chicago Press, 2007.

Sloterdijk, Peter. *Theory of the Post-War Periods*. Tr. Robert Payne. Vienna: Springer-Verlag, 2009.

Spinoza, Benedict de. *Ethics*. Tr. Edwin Curly. London: Penguin, 1996.

Sun-Tzu. *The Art of War*. Tr. John Minford. New York: Penguin Classics, 2005.

Webb, Eugene. *Worldview and Mind: Religious Thought and Psychological Development*. Columbia: University of Missouri Press, 2009.

Youcenar, Marguerite. *The Memoirs of Hadrian*. Tr. Grace Frick. New York: Farrar, Straus and Giroux, 1988.

Index

Jean-Michel Oughourlian is Ambassador of the Sovereign Order of Malta to the Republic of Armenia and former chief of psychiatry at the American Hospital in Paris. He has served as adjunct professor of psychopolitics at the University of Southern California. He is the author of *The Puppet of Desire* (1991) and *The Genesis of Desire* (2009). He collaborated with René Girard on *Things Hidden since the Foundation of the World*.

Trevor Cribben Merrill studied literature at Yale and recently received a doctorate in French and Francophone Studies from UCLA. He spent three years as a visiting student at the Ecole normale supérieure and has co-edited a volume of essays by René Girard (*La Conversion de l'art*, Champs-Flammarion, 2010).